Leadership in America's Best Urban Schools

Leadership in America's Best Urban Schools describes and demystifies the qualities that successful leaders rely on to make a difference at all levels of urban school leadership. Grounded in research, this volume reveals the multiple challenges that real urban elementary, middle, and high schools face as well as the catalysts for improvement. This insightful resource explores the critical leadership characteristics found in high-performing urban schools and gives leaders the tools to move their schools to higher levels of achievement for all students—but especially for those who are low-income, English-language learners, and from various racial and ethnic backgrounds. In shining a light on the essential qualities for exceptional leadership at all levels of urban schools, this book is a valuable guide for all educators and administrators to nurture, influence, support, and sustain excellence and equity at their schools.

Joseph F. Johnson, Jr. is Dean of the College of Education, Executive Director of the National Center for Urban School Transformation, and the QUALCOMM Professor of Urban Education at San Diego State University, USA.

Cynthia L. Uline is Professor Emeritus of Educational Leadership and Director of National Center for the 21st Century Schoolhouse at San Diego State University, USA.

Lynne G. Perez is Deputy Director of the National Center for Urban School Transformation at San Diego State University, USA.

Other EYE ON EDUCATION
Books Available from Routledge

(www.routledge.com/eyeoneducation)

Leadership for Green Schools: Sustainability for Our Children, Our Communities, and Our Planet Lisa A. W. Kensler and Cynthia L. Uline

College for Every Student: A Practitioner's Guide to Building College and Career Readiness Rick Dalton and Edward P. St. John

What Successful Principals Do! 199 Tips for Principals, Second Edition Franzy Fleck

The Revitalized Tutoring Center: A Guide to Transforming School Culture Jeremy Koselak and Brad Lyall

7 Ways to Transform the Lives of Wounded Students Joe Hendershott

School Leadership through the Seasons: A Guide to Staying Focused and Getting Results All Year Ann T. Mausbach and Kimberly Morrison

Teaching Practices from America's Best Urban Schools: A Guide for School and Classroom Leaders Joseph Johnson, Cynthia Uline, and Lynne Perez

Distributed Leadership in Schools: A Practical Guide for Learning and Improvement John A. DeFlaminis, Mustafa Abdul-Jabbar, and Eric Yoak

Strategies for Developing and Supporting School Leaders: Stepping Stones to Great Leadership Karen L. Sanzo

Crafting the Feedback Teachers Need and Deserve: A Guide for Leaders Thomas Van Soelen

Hiring the Best Staff for Your School: How to Use Narrative to Improve Your Recruiting Process Rick Jetter

Mentoring is a Verb: Strategies for Improving College and Career Readiness Russ Olwell

The Leader's Guide to Working with Underperforming Teachers: Overcoming Marginal Teaching and Getting Results Sally Zepeda

Five Critical Leadership Practices: The Secret to High-Performing Schools Ruth C. Ash and Pat H. Hodge

Principalship A to Z, Second Edition Ronald Williamson and Barbara R. Blackburn

Leadership in America's Best Urban Schools

Joseph F. Johnson, Jr.
Cynthia L. Uline
Lynne G. Perez

Routledge
Taylor & Francis Group

NEW YORK AND LONDON

First published 2017
by Routledge
711 Third Avenue, New York, NY 10017

and by Routledge
2 Park Square, Milton Park, Abingdon, Oxon, OX14 4RN

Routledge is an imprint of the Taylor & Francis Group, an informa business

Library of Congress Cataloging-in-Publication Data
Names: Johnson, Joseph F., Jr., author. | Uline, Cynthia L., author. | Perez, Lynne G., author.
Title: Leadership in Americas best urban schools / by Joseph F. Johnson, Jr, Cynthia L. Uline, and Lynne G. Perez.
Description: New York : Routledge, 2017.
Identifiers: LCCN 2016039727 | ISBN 9781138922815 (hardback) | ISBN 9781138922822 (pbk.) | ISBN 9781315685519 (master ebook) | ISBN 9781317412373 (mobi/kindle)
Subjects: LCSH: Urban schools—United States—Administration. | Educational leadership—United States. | Education, Urban—United States.
Classification: LCC LC5131 .J647 2017 | DDC 371.2—dc23
LC record available at https://lccn.loc.gov/2016039727

ISBN: 978-1-138-92281-5 (hbk)
ISBN: 978-1-138-92282-2 (pbk)
ISBN: 978-1-315-68551-9 (ebk)

Typeset in Palatino
by Apex CoVantage, LLC

Contents

Illustrations

Figures

Table

Acknowledgments

This book exists only because there are outstanding teachers, administrators, and support staff who have defied the odds and created outstanding urban schools. Not only do we respect, acknowledge, and appreciate your impressive work, but we also appreciate your willingness to open your schools to us and allow us to learn from your work. We hope this book is an affirmation of your impressive accomplishments, as well as a source of motivation as you continue to strive for excellence.

We also acknowledge and appreciate the many individuals—including school administrators, graduate students, professors, and teachers—who have engaged with us in visiting and studying America's high-performing urban schools. Your time, energy, and insights have been priceless, as we have sought to better understand teaching and learning in outstanding urban schools.

We must also acknowledge that the study of high-performing urban schools is not new. Our work builds upon a tradition of scholarship and inquiry started by heroic educators like Ron Edmonds, Larry Lezotte, and Wilbur Brookover and extended through the work of others such as Doug Reeves, James Scheurich, Karin Chenoweth, Mike Schmoker, Kati Haycock, Linda Skrla, Kathryn McKenzie, and others. These leaders constructed the foundation upon which this effort was built.

We especially acknowledge the strong support of San Diego State University. The former university president, Stephen Weber, and the former dean of the university's college of education, Lionel "Skip" Meno, envisioned a national center that would identify, study, and promote excellence in urban schools. They secured initial funding support from the QUALCOMM Corporation, and they creatively sought/provided other support that helped us start the National Center for Urban School Transformation (NCUST). As an expression of their commitment to urban K-12 education, the university has continued this strong support, even in difficult financial times. The advocacy and support of the current university president, Elliot Hirshman, and the current provost, Chukuka S. Enwemeka, have helped NCUST thrive and grow.

Finally, we acknowledge the time, wisdom, and commitment of our colleagues and staff at San Diego State University and at NCUST. We are honored to work with and learn from individuals who have committed themselves to supporting America's urban schools.

Meet the Authors

Joseph F. Johnson, Jr. is Dean of the College of Education, Executive Director of the National Center for Urban School Transformation, and the QUALCOMM Professor of Urban Education within the department of educational leadership at San Diego State University. He has previously served as a teacher, school and district administrator, state education agency administrator in Texas and Ohio, researcher and technical assistance provider, and U.S. Department of Education official. His research focuses upon schools that achieve remarkable academic results for diverse populations of students. His work has appeared in journals such as *Education and Urban Society, Educational Administration Quarterly, Educational Leadership, International Journal of Leadership in Education, Journal of Education for Students Placed at Risk, Phi Delta Kappan,* and *Theory into Practice.*

Cynthia L. Uline, Ph.D., is Professor Emeritus of Educational Leadership at San Diego State University. Cynthia previously served on faculty at the Ohio State University where she was an assistant and associate professor of Educational Administration from 1995 to 2005. She currently directs SDSU's National Center for the 21st Century Schoolhouse (http://go.sdsu.edu/education/schoolhouse/). Cynthia has also served as a teacher, teacher leader, state education agency administrator in Pennsylvania, and an educational consultant working with schools, school districts, city governments, state agencies, and governors' offices. She has published articles related to the improvement of social and physical learning environments, leadership for learning, and leadership preparation in journals such as *Educational Administration Quarterly, Teacher College Record, Journal of Educational Administration, Journal of School Leadership, Journal of Education for Students Placed at Risk, International Journal of Leadership in Education, Journal of Research and Development in Education, Theory into Practice,* and *Educational Leadership.*

Lynne G. Perez, Ph.D., is Deputy Director of the National Center for Urban School Transformation at San Diego State University. She also serves as a part-time lecturer with SDSU's Department of Educational Leadership. She serves as an executive coach in the Center's Advancing Principal Leadership in Urban Schools Program. Her work on school leadership issues has appeared in journals such as *Educational Administration Quarterly, Educational Leadership, Journal of Education for Students Placed at Risk, Journal of Educational Leadership, Journal of School Leadership,* and *Teacher College Record.*

Preface

Many authors have written about leadership in schools. This book is more specifically about leaders who have influenced outstanding learning results for all students, including students from various racial/ethnic backgrounds; from low-income, urban communities; and from various language backgrounds. In particular, this book is about leaders who have helped generate excellent and equitable learning results for all demographic groups of students.

Since 2006, the National Center for Urban School Transformation (NCUST) has been identifying, awarding, and studying many of the nation's highest achieving urban schools. These schools provided multiple evidences of success (e.g., state assessment scores, graduation rates, attendance rates, discipline data, English-acquisition data, course-taking patterns) for their students, in general. Additionally, the schools provided state assessment data as evidence that each racial/ethnic group served in these schools performed at levels above the average for all students throughout the state. As well, many of the schools demonstrated outstanding learning results for English learners and other groups of students who have traditionally been underserved by U.S. schools. Between 2006 and 2016, we visited, studied, and awarded 117 remarkable elementary, middle, and high schools that 1) served predominantly low-income students, 2) did not use selective admissions criteria, and 3) achieved outstanding results for every racial/ethnic group served. This book is based on what we learned from leaders in these typical schools that achieved very atypical results.

While the schools NCUST awarded varied in many ways, we consistently found outstanding leaders. Our findings are similar to those of Leithwood, Louis, Anderson, and Wahlstrom (2004), who reported, "Indeed, there are virtually no documented instances of troubled schools being turned around in the absence of intervention by talented leaders. Many other factors may contribute to such turnarounds, but leadership is the catalyst" (p. 5).

This book describes the nature of leadership in the impressive schools we have awarded and studied. We describe what these leaders do, why they do it, and how they do it consistently and effectively. As well, we attempt to distinguish the leadership found in these high-performing schools from less effective examples we have encountered at struggling schools.

Typically, we have found impressive principal leaders in these high-performing urban schools; however, it is important to note that often other leaders (including teacher leaders, counselors, and other school administrators) played important leadership roles. In fact, the principal leaders in these high-performing urban schools often created leadership opportunities for others and supported them in fulfilling those responsibilities well. Therefore, we do not limit this discussion to the leadership role of principals. Instead, we describe the leadership behaviors of the various individuals who have influenced, initiated, supported, and sustained excellence and equity at their schools.

Intended Audience

This book is about leaders who are committed to generating excellent and equitable learning results for their students. Similarly, it is written for leaders who are committed to generating excellent and equitable learning results for their students. We expect that this book will be useful to principals, assistant principals, deans, superintendents, area superintendents, executive directors, principal supervisors, and many other school and district administrators. As well, we expect this book to be helpful to teacher leaders with many different job titles (such as lead teacher, department chair, resource teacher, helping teacher, team leader, resource specialist, teacher on specialist assignment, math specialist, reading specialist, science specialist, or technology specialist) and teacher leaders with no title at all. This volume is intended to be useful to any leader (or future leader) who is striving to influence the academic success of all students and all demographic groups of students.

Finally, we hope this book will be useful to individuals who, like us, are struggling to better understand why some leaders are able to lift their schools to high levels of performance, while leaders in other schools with similar demographics and challenges work hard, yet fail to make a sustainable difference on any measurable outcomes. We hope that our findings influence further study of schools that achieve excellent and equitable learning results so that, as a profession, we continuously improve our support of leaders who are committed to transforming their schools and districts so that all children achieve academic excellence, develop and sustain a love of learning, and graduate well prepared to succeed in post-secondary education, the workplace, and their communities.

Contents of the Book

This book is divided into two parts. The first part provides a detailed description of the schools we studied. There are many myths about practices in high-performing urban schools. Most of the myths emanate from schools that did not achieve multiple evidences of educational success for diverse populations of students. Often, the myths come from schools that were not able to sustain successes for longer than one or two years. Throughout Part I, we have endeavored to provide a rich description of what we found in the high-performing urban schools we identified, awarded, and studied. We believe that if leaders (at either the district, school, or classroom level) are likely to support the pursuit of excellence and equity, they must have a clear and accurate picture of the salient characteristics of excellent and equitable schools. It is hard to re-create something while guessing what it looks like.

To help the reader understand what the schools we studied look like, we have first endeavored to explain the data that lead us to determine that these schools have achieved excellent and equitable learning results. In Chapter 1, we explain the process NCUST uses for identifying National Excellence in Urban Education Award winners. The NCUST award criteria were designed to help ensure that we identified schools that were achieving both excellent and equitable results. In addition to explaining the criteria, Chapter 1 provides a deeper examination of the drive for excellence and equity we found in classrooms, teacher collaboration meetings, professional development discussions, and other interactions in the high-performing schools studied.

From our first visits to these schools, we noticed forces that influenced the impressive learning results we found. In particular, we noticed a core of empowering school characteristics that provided a stark contrast to the characteristics of more typical urban schools. It is important to note that these characteristics are neither new nor unique. In fact, to some extent they can be found in at least one or two classrooms in every school. This book, however, is about schools where these characteristics have become the norm. Leaders have influenced people and shaped systems and structures so that these characteristics define their schools.

In the strongest schools, we found that these empowering characteristics were nurtured and developed systematically. They did not emerge accidentally. Structures, routines, norms, and patterns of operation were established to help ensure that the three characteristics would be nurtured and grow over time. Throughout Chapters 2, 3, and 4 we describe the structures, routines, policies, and norms that worked together to create a coherent educational improvement system that promoted the development of the empowering characteristics—for example, in Chapter 2, as we describe the first empowering characteristic as a positive, transformational culture. In the same chapter, we also describe how structures, routines, policies, and norms worked systematically to produce this learning culture where all stakeholders (including students, families, and educators) perceived the school as a safe and caring environment, where they were valued and respected, and where they felt capable of success. We want the reader to understand what a positive transformation culture looks like and how it is different from the culture found in most schools. Additionally, however, we want readers to understand that such a culture does not occur automatically when a school acquires a visible, caring, and/or charismatic principal. Meaningful school-wide change requires systemic change. So, in Chapters 2, 3, and 4, we include sections that focus on the power of a coherent educational improvement system.

From our early visits, we knew that leaders played a major role in helping bring about the improvements that generated great results in high-performing urban schools. In Part II of this book, we give special attention to articulating the nature of the leadership that influenced the establishment of a positive transformational culture, rigorous curricula, and effective instruction, while laying the foundation for equitable and excellent learning results for all students. Chapters 5 through 8 focus upon the key leadership challenges that influenced success in high-performing urban schools. These findings add to and build upon the literature on leadership in effective schools (Aleman, Johnson, & Perez, 2009; Barth et al., 1999; Cotton, 2003; Grady, Wayson, & Zirkel, 1989; Johnson, Lein, & Ragland, 1998; Marzano, Waters, & McNulty, 2005; Robinson, 2011).

Each chapter (1 through 8) includes a section entitled "What It Is & What It Isn't." Readers of *Teaching Practices from America's Best Urban Schools* (Johnson, Perez, & Uline, 2012) found that this feature provided useful examples of the concepts we sought to convey. By distinguishing "what it is" from "what it isn't," we endeavor to reduce confusion around educational rhetoric and help readers focus on the most salient issues.

Also, each chapter includes a brief self-assessment tool. This tool is designed to help leaders assess their current performance. This information might be useful as leaders attempt to gauge their progress and refine their efforts to influence excellence and equity in their schools.

With each visit to the high-performing urban schools we awarded, we gained renewed hope for urban education in the United States. We were inspired by the accomplishments of educators who created learning environments to which we would be happy sending our grandchildren. We acquired a deeper appreciation of the complexities involved in negotiating multi-layered bureaucracies, addressing the challenges of urban communities, and confronting pervasive, counter-productive conceptualizations of school culture, curricula, and instruction. Simultaneously, however, we developed a deeper understanding of the roles leaders play in working with teachers, students, parents, support personnel, and other administrators to influence practices, structures, routines, policies, and norms that result in outstanding learning results for all groups of children. With this book, we endeavor to create a lens through which our readers might see the schools we visited. We hope readers will be similarly inspired, while at the same time appreciative of the complexities inherent in urban education. We trust they will develop a deeper understanding of how leaders can work with stakeholders to nurture excellent and equitable learning results for all of the children they have the privilege to educate.

References

Aleman, D., Johnson, J. F., & Perez, L. (2009). Winning schools for English language learners. *Educational Leadership, 66*(7), 66–69.

Barth, P., Haycock, K., Jackson, H., Mora, K., Ruiz, P., Robinson, S., & Wilkens, A. (1999). *Dispelling the myth: High-poverty schools exceeding expectations.* Washington, DC: Council of Chief State School Officers.

Cotton, K. (2003). *Principals and student achievement: What the research says.* Arlington, VA: Association for Supervision and Curriculum Development.

Grady, M. L., Wayson, W. W., & Zirkel, P. A. (1989). A review of effective schools research as it relates to effective principals. UCEA Monograph Series. Tempe, AZ: University Council of Educational Administration (ED 304 743).

Johnson, J. F., Lein, L., & Ragland, M. (1998). Highly successful schools in communities challenged by poverty. In Y. S. George & V. V. Van Horne (Eds.), *Science education reform for all (SERA): Sustaining the science, mathematics, and technology reform* (pp. 111–116). Washington, DC: American Association for the Advancement of Science.

Johnson, J. F., Perez, L. G., & Uline, C. L. (2012). *Teaching practices from America's best urban schools: A guide for school and classroom leaders.* Larchmont, NY: Eye on Education.

Leithwood, K., Louis, K. S., Anderson, S., & Wahlstrom, K. (2004). *Review of research: How leadership influences student learning.* New York: The Wallace Foundation.

Marzano, R. J., Waters, T., & McNulty, B. A. (2005). *School leadership that works: From research to results.* Alexandria, VA: Association for Supervision and Curriculum Development.

Robinson, V. (2011). *Student-centered leadership.* San Francisco, CA: Jossey-Bass.

 # Schools that Achieve Outstanding Results for All Students

Many researchers, including Chenoweth and Theokas (2011), Cotton (2003), Hallinger and Heck (1996), Leithwood, Louis, Anderson, and Wahlstrom (2004), and Murphy and Torre (2015), have emphasized the importance of the leader's vision in influencing significant change in schools. Whenever district, school, or classroom leaders have successfully influenced major changes, it is because they envisioned both the results that were needed and the changes necessary to pursue and achieve those results. Also, they led other key stakeholders to share, embrace, and strive toward the same vision.

Part I of this book is intended to help the reader envision typical urban schools achieving outstanding results for each demographic group they serve. We want the reader to understand and envision the impressive results associated with the pursuit of both academic excellence and equity, as found in the schools we studied. Blankstein and Noguera (2015) explained that the pursuit of equity is often perceived as zero-sum thinking (doing more for one group at the expense of another) and is often perceived as incompatible with the pursuit of excellence. To the contrary, they suggested that "equity and excellence are not at odds, and that the highest level of excellence will actually be obtained through the pursuit of equity" (Blankstein & Noguera, 2015, p. 5). Part I of this book is designed to help the reader see what we saw both in school performance data, as well as in observations of classrooms, collaboration meetings, playgrounds, hallways, and other school events that reflected the simultaneous pursuit of excellence and equity.

Additionally, Part I is written to enable the reader to envision the school characteristics that were necessary in order to achieve excellence and equity. Even though the schools we studied differed in grade-level configurations, enrollments, geographic regions, administrative structures, racial/ethnic populations, expenditure levels, and many other factors, they all developed cultures, curricula, and instructional practices that empowered their pursuit of excellence and equity. We want the reader to understand and envision the deep changes that may be necessary in order to transform struggling urban schools. As well, we want readers to envision the subtle aspects of culture, curricula, and instruction that may distinguish success from frustration.

Chapter 1 provides a detailed discussion of the excellent and equitable results found in the high-performing schools we studied. Then, Chapters 2, 3, and 4 describe the culture, curricula, and instructional practices that empowered the pursuit of excellent and equitable learning results.

References

Blankstein, A.M., & Noguera, P. (2015). *Excellence through equity: Five principles of courageous leadership to guide achievement for every student.* Thousand Oaks, CA: Corwin.

Chenoweth, K., & Theokas, C. (2011). *Getting it done: Leading academic success in unexpected schools.* Cambridge, MA: Harvard Education Press.

Cotton, K. (2003). *Principals and student achievement: What the research says.* Arlington, VA: Association for Supervision and Curriculum Development.

Hallinger, P., & Heck, R. (1996). Reassessing the principal's role in school effectiveness: A review of empirical research, 1980–1995. *Educational Administration Quarterly, 32*(1), 5–44.

Leithwood, K., Louis, K.S., Anderson, S., & Wahlstrom, K. (2004). *Review of research: How leadership influences student learning.* New York: The Wallace Foundation.

Murphy, J., & Torre, D. (2015). Vision: Essential scaffolding. *Educational Management Administration and Leadership, 43*(2), 177–197.

Excellent and Equitable Learning Results

People considered this a rough school. Frequently, there were fights. Academics were not a priority. When I was offered the principalship, I turned it down at first. Why would I want to waste my career in this type of setting? But the superintendent kept pushing me to take the job. Finally, I agreed to take it, but only with the intent of making this one of the best schools in the state. I think the superintendent thought I was a jerk for not wanting to take the job initially. Then the superintendent probably thought I was delusional for believing the school could become one of the best schools in the state. But I was serious. I wanted this to be a school where anyone would be happy to send their kid, regardless of race or income. I wanted to win. I wanted all of these kids to win and win big. That's why I'm here.

Kevin Grawer, Principal, Maplewood Richmond
Heights High, St. Louis, MO

In the United States, it is remarkably easy to predict school attendance rates, reading performance, course passage rates, performance on state achievement tests, school suspension rates, enrollment in advanced classes, graduation rates, college attendance rates, or almost any other important academic outcome simply by knowing five student variables: race/ethnicity, language background, family income, gender, and zip code. Huge gaps in achievement, associated with these variables, challenge our cities and states and pose significant threats to our social and economic wellbeing. In contrast, there are outstanding schools that defy these patterns, schools where one cannot reliably predict learning outcomes based on any demographic characteristic, schools where achievement gaps have been minimized or eliminated. This book is about the nature of leadership in these impressive schools.

In mathematics, a theory is proven false when someone identifies just one case in which the theory is not true. The one case that proves the theory false is called an existence proof. The fact that this one case exists proves the theory wrong. In the 1960s, researchers determined that schools had little impact on student achievement after socio-economic variables were considered (Coleman et al., 1966). They concluded that issues beyond the control of schools (e.g., poverty, race, and parental education levels) had greater influence on learning results than the actions of educators. In response to the Coleman Report, researchers identified *effective schools* that produced achievement results that were substantially better than the results achieved at other schools that served similar demographic populations (Brookover & Lezotte, 1979; Brookover & Schneider, 1975; Edmonds, 1979; Lightfoot, 1981; Venezky & Winfield, 1979; Weber, 1971). If the quality of schools did not influence student achievement because of the overwhelming power of socio-economic variables, then how could some schools demonstrate substantially better results than other schools that served similar demographic populations? Each effective school was an existence proof that poked holes in the Coleman Report's findings and conclusions.

Today, in an era where schools are being challenged to teach rigorous academic standards to all groups of students, there are some who contend that schools cannot simultaneously achieve excellence and equity. They suggest that the best that can be done in schools that serve predominantly Latino, Black, Native American, English learners or low-income students is to pursue equity in the form of better than typical results, similar to the results described in effective school studies. Alternately, some suggest that school districts should separate small groups of the highest achieving students and provide separate curricula or even separate schools so that "excellence" can be achieved for the capable few. The schools that are the focus of this book are today's existence proofs, refuting these approaches. Each of these schools has demonstrated that excellence and equity can be simultaneously pursued and attained. Without resorting to selective admissions, schools can achieve outstanding academic results (far beyond overall state averages) for every demographic group served. This chapter explains the evidence of excellent and equitable learning results we found in the schools we awarded and studied.

Since 2006, the National Center for Urban School Transformation (NCUST) at San Diego State University has been identifying, celebrating, and learning from high-performing elementary, middle, and high schools. Each year, the Center publishes and disseminates a set of award criteria (See Appendix A); solicits nominations from state superintendents, local urban superintendents, and leaders of schools that won various national and state-level distinctions; and begins a rigorous process of identifying schools for the Center's National Excellence in Urban Education Award. From the beginning, the award program was designed to identify schools that achieved both excellent and equitable learning results. We wanted to award schools that demonstrated a variety of learning results that exceeded state averages. We looked for urban schools with learning results (e.g., student success rates, graduation rates, state assessment scores, attendance rates) that were comparable to the results achieved in respected suburban schools. At the same time, we insisted that award winners demonstrate considerable evidence of high rates of academic success for all demographic groups they served, specifically students of color and students from families who met low-income criteria. Some of the schools awarded might be considered turnaround schools, because they improved dramatically over a short period of time. Other award-winning schools had a long history of impressive academic successes.

Schools could not earn the National Excellence in Urban Education Award simply by achieving strong overall learning results. Instead, schools were also required to provide evidence that every racial/ethnic/income group served was achieving at rates that exceeded state averages. We sought to identify, award, and study schools that evidenced both excellence and equity in learning results. This focus on both equity and excellence makes the National Excellence in Urban Education Award different from many other award programs. For example, some programs focus solely on measures of excellence without attention to the levels of attainment of the diverse groups of students served. As well, some award programs focus solely on schools that demonstrate impressive progress for diverse populations of students. Also, some award programs (like the National Blue Ribbon Schools Program) include two separate and distinct programs, one focused on excellence (high rates of academic attainment), and one focused on equity (growth for diverse populations of students). In contrast, NCUST has sought to award and study urban schools with evidence of both excellence and equity in student learning outcomes.

Evidence of Excellence and Equity

The schools NCUST awarded and studied varied in many ways. For example, the size of the awarded schools varied. Some of the awarded schools are small, serving only 100 to 400 students. The smaller schools included charter schools, career pathway high schools, and small neighborhood schools. In contrast, NCUST also awarded large elementary and middle schools serving 1,000 to 1,800 students. In addition, NCUST has awarded some large comprehensive high schools serving more than 2,000 students. School size has never been a selection criterion. Instead, NCUST has been open to the possibility that schools can create equitable and excellent learning opportunities, regardless of the size of the student population.

In addition, the schools varied in grade configurations. The majority of schools awarded have been elementary schools; however, NCUST has awarded elementary, middle, and high schools with varying grade configurations. Even though schools presented different challenges, programs, and practices, all of the schools presented strong evidence that they were achieving excellent and equitable learning results.

In order to apply for the award, schools had to demonstrate that they served large percentages of students who typically were not served well in public schools. First, schools had to be situated in urban areas. We required that each school be in an area designated by the U.S. Census Bureau as a metropolitan statistical area. These areas have populations of at least 50,000 residents. This broad definition allowed us to consider schools that were in inner-ring suburbs such as Maplewood, Missouri (next to St. Louis) or Revere, Massachusetts (next to Boston). As well, award winners have included many schools in typical big-city urban districts such as the Chicago Public Schools, the Houston Independent School District, the Los Angeles Unified School District, the Cleveland Metropolitan School District, and the Metropolitan Nashville Public Schools.

Some might think that this book does not apply to their school or district, because they are not located within an "urban" area. While the schools discussed in this book all met the urban criteria described above, urbanicity is only one of the challenges these schools had to overcome. The book is about schools that overcame a variety of challenges to achieve educational excellence and equity. The book should be considered a resource to any educator who is committed to the pursuit of outstanding learning results for every demographic group of students they serve.

To ensure that applicant schools were grappling with and overcoming the real challenges associated with educating typical urban students, applicants were required to ensure they did not use admissions policies that allowed them to select students with better academic records or potential or reject students with fewer academic qualifications. NCUST disqualified schools that required students to take entrance tests or maintain certain grade-point averages. Magnet schools or charter schools could apply only if they accepted students on a first-come, first-served basis or if they used lotteries and/or attendance areas to determine which students would be enrolled. Of course, this restriction eliminated many outstanding schools from our consideration. However, by excluding schools with selective admission policies we helped ensure that the schools we identified were achieving atypical learning results for typical urban students.

The majority of schools awarded have been typical public schools that serve students who live in the neighborhood surrounding the school; however, approximately 11 percent of the schools awarded have been charter schools. To identify schools that truly achieved excellence and equity, NCUST sought to ensure that students were not denied enrollment on the basis of academic performance.

It is also important to note that applicants had to serve predominantly low-income communities. In elementary schools, at least 60 percent of the students had to qualify for the federal free- or reduced-price meal program. Often students in secondary schools are reluctant to apply for free-meal programs (even though they may not be more affluent than their siblings in elementary school). Consequently, we considered middle schools if at least 50 percent of the students met the low-income criteria, and we considered high schools if at least 40 percent of the students met low-income criteria. Even with these lenient criteria, in most of the schools NCUST awarded, over 75 percent of the students served met the income criteria for the federal free- or reduced-price meal program.

School Effectiveness Criteria

Applicants for the National Excellence in Urban Education Award were required to meet multiple criteria related to excellence and equity (not just good test scores). For example, NCUST looked carefully at attendance rates, graduation rates, participation in advanced courses of study, suspension/expulsion rates, college entrance exam scores, and a variety of other indicators. For many indicators, applicants had to present data for the entire school population served, as well as data for each demographic group served. Applicants had to show that they maintained average daily attendance rates of at least 92 percent. They had to demonstrate very low suspension rates for all students, and for every demographic group they served. High schools had to demonstrate strong graduation rates for all students, and for every demographic group they served.

Results from state standardized tests were a critical determinant for many schools. Applicants were required to demonstrate that a higher percentage of their students achieved proficient or advanced academic levels than the statewide percentage of students who achieved proficient or advanced levels. On at least half of the tests administered for state accountability purposes, the school had to perform at or higher than the state average for two consecutive years.

Additionally, schools were required to show evidence of strong academic accomplishment for every racial/ethnic group of students they served. For each demographic group served, the school was required to demonstrate that the percentage of students performing at the proficient or advanced level was equal to or higher than the statewide percentage of all students who performed at those levels. Schools were required to demonstrate this high level of achievement on at least two state assessments. Please note that NCUST compared each demographic group to the statewide performance of all students, not simply the statewide performance of students in the same demographic group. This requirement eliminated many schools from consideration. For example, some schools performed very well compared to state averages; however, when achievement results were disaggregated, one or more racial/ethnic group(s) performed lower than the statewide averages in all subject areas.

NCUST also required applicants to present strong evidence of academic success for English learners and students with disabilities. Applicants had to demonstrate that English learners were developing greater proficiency in the use of the English language, as well as greater proficiency in academic areas. Schools also had to show data related to the academic progress of students with disabilities. In several winning schools, such as Mary Walke Stephens Elementary in Houston's Aldine Independent School District or Cerritos Elementary in the Glendale Unified School District in California, the percentage of English learners who achieved proficiency on state assessments exceeded the overall statewide percentage of students who achieved proficiency. In sum, in order to qualify for the National Excellence in Urban Education Award, schools were required to demonstrate evidence of academic excellence for every demographic group they served.

The Selection Process

Each year, many schools make inquiries about the National Excellence in Urban Education Awards. School and district personnel call with questions regarding the award criteria or attend the Center's free webinars regarding the application process. Often, these interactions result in school leaders determining that they do not qualify for the award program. Typically, applicants include 50 to 60 elementary, middle, and high schools. Applicants have included many National Blue Ribbon Schools, National Title I Distinguished Schools, schools recognized on *U.S. News & World Report's Best High Schools in America*, and schools that earned a wide array of statewide distinctions.

In order to apply, schools completed an application. Most of the application information focused upon quantitative data related to the award criteria (e.g., percentages of students meeting low-income criteria, average daily attendance percentages, percentages of students who performed at the proficient or advanced levels on state assessments, graduation rates, suspension rates, numbers of students in advanced classes). The applications provided schools limited opportunities to write narrative descriptions of their schools. By limiting the writing required, NCUST hoped to minimize the time school leaders had to spend preparing the application. As well, NCUST hoped to focus eligibility primarily on results achieved for diverse populations of students.

In addition to submitting an application, schools submitted a DVD with video recordings of two lessons. Schools were required to send video clips (between 10 to 30 minutes in length) featuring some of their best examples of instruction. The video recordings provided additional perspective on curricular rigor, instructional effectiveness, and the climate and culture of the school.

After reviewing the applications, NCUST selected, as finalists, the schools that presented the strongest evidence of academic success for all demographic groups of students. Schools that met all eligibility criteria, but were not selected as finalists, were listed on the Center's website as honor roll schools.

We conducted on-site visits to every finalist school. Teams of researchers, teachers, and administrators (including educators from previous winning schools) visited each finalist. Team members spent considerable amounts of time observing classrooms; interviewing teachers, administrators, counselors, students, and parents; and reviewing student work. With the permission of the interviewees, team members made audio recordings of the interviews and video recordings of some of the administrator interviews. Additionally, the teams observed teacher planning meetings, parent meetings, and staff meetings. They talked with district administrators and neighborhood leaders.

During our site visits, we noted evidence of the pursuit of excellent and equitable learning results beyond the impressive application data the schools submitted. For example, we noted that school personnel structured programs and services to ensure that English learners were being taught the same challenging academic content provided to native English speakers. We found that assignments required students to think deeply about academic standards in ways that required the application of higher order thinking skills. We observed teacher collaboration teams pushing themselves to design lessons that would intrigue and engage Black, Latino, and low-income students. We watched special education personnel work in general education classrooms to help ensure that students with disabilities progressed toward mastering the same academic standards all other students learned. We heard students from low-income families describe the many ways that teachers and administrators had helped them feel accepted, respected, and valued. As well, students shared how their relationships with school personnel positively influenced their motivation to work hard and excel.

By visiting and observing all classrooms in each finalist school, we affirmed that all students (regardless of demographic groups) were receiving access to challenging academic standards. By interviewing students and parents, we learned that the schools had developed cultures that helped all students believe that they had the opportunity to graduate, pursue postsecondary education, and succeed in meaningful careers. By interviewing large samples of teachers and administrators (like the principal of Maplewood Richmond Heights High School quoted at the beginning of this chapter), we acquired evidence that educators were relentlessly striving to create learning conditions that ensured the success of all students and every demographic group of students they served. Equity and excellence were not merely slogans, random workshop topics, or bullet points buried within official school plans. Instead, the pursuit of excellent and equitable learning results was the underlying purpose for practically every activity, program, routine, and policy.

Over the past 10 years, NCUST refined observation and interview protocols so that we might learn more about the practices that influenced excellent and equitable learning results in high-performing urban schools. We endeavored to probe deeper to understand how leaders initiated changes, generated stakeholder commitment, managed setbacks, and sustained momentum.

Each year, after all site visits were completed, team leaders met to compare detailed notes from visits. The schools selected as award winners were those where team members found the most evidence of curricular rigor, instructional effectiveness, positive relationships, and focus on continuous improvement. Between 2006 and 2015, NCUST awarded 117 schools from 21 states and Washington, DC (see Appendix B for the full list of award winners). Beginning in 2012, NCUST differentiated winners as bronze-, silver-, and gold-award recipients.

Additionally, apart from our award program, we conducted phone interviews and face-to-face interviews with selected teachers and administrators from these impressive schools. Our doctoral students engaged in in-depth case studies of several of the winning schools. And, we continue to examine data, identify themes, discuss conclusions, seek additional evidence, and deepen our understandings. These efforts continue to focus on developing deeper understandings of the factors that contribute to excellence and equity in these schools.

Leadership for Excellence and Equity

Results did not emerge by chance. In fact, leaders influenced the design of their schools such that excellent and equitable results were likely, even inevitable.

This book focuses specifically and exclusively on leadership that influenced educational excellence and equity. Other books, reports, and articles focus on school leadership in general or school leadership that resulted in other outcomes. Here, however, we have focused on the role leaders played in influencing outstanding educational results for all demographic groups of students. A growing body of research and scholarship (Bogotch, 2002; Dantley & Tillman, 2006; DeMatthews, 2015; Furman, 2012; Jean-Marie, 2008; Marshall & Ward, 2004; Scheurich & Skrla, 2003; Theoharis, 2009) frames these leadership commitments in terms of social justice, with school leaders "mak[ing] issues of race, class, gender, disability, sexual orientation, and other historically and currently marginalizing conditions in the United States central to their advocacy, leadership practice, and vision" (Theoharis, 2007, p. 223). These social justice leaders demonstrate an unfailing commitment to equity and justice that motivates and informs their efforts to raise student achievement, improve school structures, re-center (toward social justice outcomes) and enhance staff capacity, and strengthen school culture and community (Theoharis, 2009). Whether or not school leaders identified themselves as social justice leaders, leaders in the schools we studied demonstrated the same unfailing commitment to equity and justice as they sought to improve programs, policies, and practices that influenced learning results for all demographic groups of students.

Paul Batalden wrote, "Every system is perfectly designed to get the results it gets" (Carr, 2008). While one can argue that public education systems in the United States are perfectly designed to achieve the results they get, we are convinced that the high-performing urban schools we identified and studied were perfectly designed to achieve excellent and equitable learning results. Results did not emerge by chance. In fact, leaders influenced the design of their schools such that excellent and equitable results were likely, even inevitable.

Leaders promoted the attainment of excellent and equitable learning results by helping teachers and other stakeholders establish a few key school characteristics. The key school characteristics developed as a result of a coherent educational

Figure 1.1. **Layers of Findings**

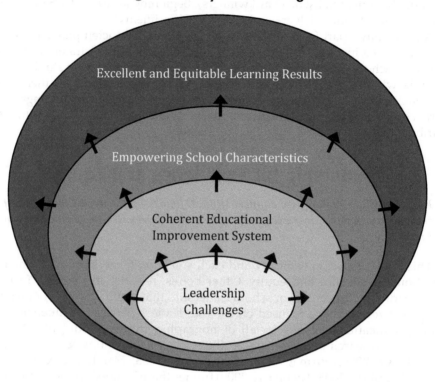

improvement system. In order to establish a coherent educational improvement system that would lead ultimately to excellent and equitable learning results, leaders had to overcome some specific, powerful leadership challenges. Figure 1.1 illustrates how these factors interrelate and influence the attainment of excellent and equitable learning results.

Establishing the Right School Characteristics

As we visited, studied, and learned more about the high-performing schools we identified, we came to understand that the excellent and equitable learning results we found were predictable outcomes of a few essential school characteristics. These school characteristics empowered or fueled the pursuit of excellent and equitable learning results. In particular, we noticed that these empowering school characteristics provided a stark contrast to the characteristics of more typical urban schools. It is important to note that these characteristics are neither new nor unique. In fact, to some extent they can be found in at least one or two classrooms in every school. In high-performing urban schools, however, these characteristics have become the norm. Leaders have influenced people and shaped systems and structures so that these characteristics define their schools.

The first of these characteristics is a *positive transformational culture*. Consistently, we found that high-performing urban schools exhibited a culture that was positive and supportive for all students, parents, teachers, and other school personnel. At the same time, the culture promoted a shared sense of urgency for growth and improvement in teaching and learning for all students. This positive transformational culture is described in Chapter 2.

The second empowering school characteristic is *access to challenging academic curricula*. The nature of what was taught was substantially more rigorous, with a greater focus on building the depth of student understanding, than what was taught in more typical urban schools. In the high-performing schools, educators endeavored to ensure that all students (and all demographic groups of students) had access to challenging curricula. This second characteristic is described in Chapter 3.

The third characteristic focuses on the nature of instruction. As described in Chapter 4, teachers in high-performing schools provided *effective instruction that resulted in high rates of student engagement and mastery*. Educators worked deliberately and persistently to refine their instructional approaches in ways that resulted in all students (and all groups of students) engaging in learning and achieving mastery of key concepts and skills.

Creating a Coherent Educational Improvement System

Through our study of the high-performing schools, we also learned that the empowering school characteristics did not emerge by purchasing a program, attending a workshop, or relying on a principal's charisma. Instead, they were the intended results of a coherent educational improvement system. Whereas in more typical schools we often find a multitude of disjointed systems that do not necessarily complement each other, we consistently found that high-performing urban schools benefit from a coherent educational improvement system that helps them develop, sustain, and grow the culture, curricula, and instruction needed to generate excellent and equitable learning.

As illustrated in Figure 1.2, the coherent educational improvement system at each school includes elements that facilitate five interrelated outcomes. For example, when structures, routines, policies, and norms help all stakeholders feel valued and capable, there is a systemic impact on the other four outcomes. Similarly, when stakeholders share a common focus on a set of challenging concepts and skills, there is a systemic impact on all of the other outcomes. The five outcomes of a coherent educational improvement system include the following:

1) **Stakeholders feel valued and capable.** All stakeholders perceive the school as a safe and caring environment, where they are valued and respected, and where they feel capable of success. Structures, routines, policies, and norms help all groups of students perceive that educators respect, value, and appreciate them as individuals. Students perceive that the adults care about them and are committed to their immediate and long-term success. Students enjoy being at school. They believe that school personnel care enough to help ensure their academic success and their success in life. Similarly, parents/families and community members feel respected as important partners in the education of their children. They perceive that school personnel value their small and large contributions to their children's education and wellbeing. Parents perceive hope for their children's academic future.

Figure 1.2. Coherent Educational Improvement System

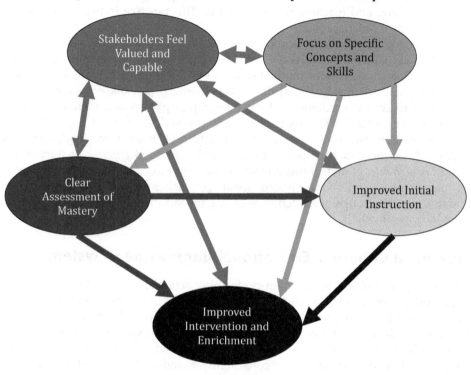

Additionally, structures, routines, policies, and norms help school personnel (including teachers, counselors, paraprofessionals, clerical staff, custodians, and others who work at the school) perceive that their administrators and colleagues care about them, value their contributions, and are committed to their professional success.

2) **Educators develop a focus on teaching a set of important, challenging concepts and skills to mastery.** Structures, routines, policies, and norms help teachers and administrators generate common understandings of *what* students should know and be able to accomplish as they progress through each grade and each major subject area. Teachers have specified the key concepts and skills students need to master. As well, they have specified the depth of knowledge students should be able to demonstrate. Educators have also specified the timeline by which mastery should occur.

3) **Educators develop clarity about how they will assess student mastery of key concepts and skills**. Structures, routines, policies, and norms help teachers and administrators reach agreement on *how* and *when* they will assess mastery of the key concepts and skills they believe students should learn. Teachers develop or adopt common assessments and administer the assessments in similar timeframes and in similar ways. It is unlikely that one teacher would label student

work as acceptable if a colleague teacher would label similar work as unacceptably below the standard.

4) **Educators continuously improve the effectiveness of initial instruction.** Structures, routines, policies, and norms result in teachers designing and providing a quality of instruction that results in almost all students (and all demographic groups of students) achieving mastery after initial instruction. High-quality initial instruction is a result of the synergy among the following:

a. Frequent and regular collaborative planning that helps teachers design lessons that are likely to lead all demographic groups of students to mastery of the content taught;

b. Frequent and regular classroom observations and feedback that support teachers as they endeavor to improve the extent to which all students demonstrate mastery; and

c. Focused professional development (based on needs identified through classroom observations and the collaborative analysis of student learning results) that helps teachers more effectively plan initial instruction.

5) **Educators continuously improve the effectiveness of intervention and enrichment.** Structures, routines, policies, and norms result in the development, implementation, evaluation, and refinement of interventions when students do not demonstrate the mastery of standards as a result of initial instruction. Even when students demonstrate mastery after initial instruction, structures, routines, policies, and norms result in the development of further enriching learning experiences that help students attain deeper levels of understanding. These responses to initial instruction are strongly influenced by collaborative examinations of student work, classroom observations and feedback, and professional development.

Addressing Leadership Challenges

We also learned that it is not easy for leaders to establish the essential school characteristics or to develop a coherent educational improvement system that yields the desired outcomes. As NCUST was identifying, awarding, and studying high-performing urban schools, we were simultaneously entering into agreements with urban school districts to help them support principals and their leadership teams in emulating the key characteristics and educational improvement system elements we found in the schools we were studying. We learned that a host of leadership challenges make it difficult to institute these sometimes subtle, yet often dramatic, changes in schools. Through in-depth interviews with principals and other school leaders in the high-performing schools, we developed a deeper understanding of the leadership challenges that frequently frustrate progress. As well, we learned more about how leaders in our award-winning schools addressed and overcame these challenges. This information is presented in Part II (specifically Chapters 5, 6, 7, and 8).

Summary

We cannot pursue equity without attending to excellence. We cannot successfully achieve excellence without a powerful commitment to equity. Equity without excellence is nothing more than mediocrity. Excellence without equity is an oxymoron.

School district, state, and national data affirm the pervasive nature of achievement gaps in America's public schools. On the other hand, if throughout the nation Black students performed at levels comparable to the achievement of Black students at West Manor Elementary in Atlanta, Georgia; at Dandy Middle School in Fort Lauderdale, Florida; or at Mallard Creek High School in Charlotte, North Carolina, the Black/White achievement gap would be minimized or eliminated. If throughout the nation Latino students performed at levels comparable to the achievement of Latino students at Finney Elementary in the Chula Vista Elementary School District near San Diego; at Eastwood Middle School in El Paso's Ysleta Independent School District; or at MacArthur Senior High School in Houston's Aldine Independent School District, the Latino/White achievement gap would vanish. Gaps related to race/ethnicity, language background, family income, gender, and zip code would largely vanish if public schools throughout the nation achieved results similar to the results achieved at the schools that are the focus of this book.

These schools teach us that excellence and equity are not competing goals. Instead, equity and excellence are essential components of the same phenomenon. We cannot pursue equity without attending to excellence. We cannot successfully achieve excellence without a powerful commitment to equity. Equity without excellence is nothing more than mediocrity. Excellence without equity is an oxymoron.

What It Is & What It Isn't: Excellent and Equitable Learning Results

What It Is: High Levels of Success for Every Demographic Group

Every demographic group served at the school achieves at levels higher than the overall average of students in the state. Example: 62% of Black students, 61% of Latino students, and 63% of students who qualify for free- or reduced-price lunch, 62% of males, 62% of females, and 59% of English learners at Smith High performed at the proficient or advanced level on the state's mathematics assessment. Statewide, only 58% of all high school students performed at the proficient or advanced level on the state mathematics assessment. (In every school described in this book, every demographic group of students served performed at levels on state assessments that exceeded overall averages.)

What It Isn't: High Levels of Success on Average (but Not for All)

Each demographic group served at the school achieves at levels higher than the average for the specific demographic group statewide; however, the achievement of the students in each demographic group served falls short of the overall performance of all students in the state. Example: 52% of Black students, 53% of Latino students, and 51% of students who qualify for free- or reduced-price lunch at John Doe High performed at the proficient or advanced level on the state's English assessment. Statewide only 40% of Black students, 41% of Latino students, and 43%

of students receiving free- or reduced-price meals performed at the proficient or advanced level in English. However, overall, 59% of high school students in the state performed at the proficient or advanced level. (NCUST did not include schools in which demographic groups compared well with the same demographic group state-wide, but performed less than the overall averages for all students in the state.)

* * *

What It is: Multiple Evidences of Excellence Regardless of Demographics

Using any specific indicator of academic achievement (e.g., the percentage of third-grade students reading at grade level, the number of high school credits earned by the end of the ninth grade, the number of students passing advanced placement tests, the percentage of school days attended, the percentage of eighth graders mastering algebra I), one cannot accurately predict how well students at the school performed simply by knowing the race/ethnicity, language background, family income level, gender, or zip code of students.

What It Isn't: Demographics Predict Destiny

Using any specific indicator of academic achievement, one can reasonably predict how well students at the school performed simply by knowing the race/ethnicity, language background, family income level, gender, or zip code of students.

* * *

What It Is: Typical Students Achieving Atypical Results

Every demographic group served at the middle school achieves at levels higher than the overall average of students in the state on multiple measures *and* the school enrolls all students who live in the district's attendance area on a first-come, first-served basis. (Each school described in this book did not use admissions policies that allowed them to select students with better academic records or potential or reject students with fewer academic qualifications.)

What It Isn't: Atypical Students Achieving Atypical Results

Each demographic group served at the middle school achieves at levels higher than the overall average of students in the state on multiple measures; however, students were required to take an entrance test and submit prior report cards. Students who performed poorly on the entrance test or who had low report card grades were less likely to be enrolled.

School Self-Assessment Tool: Is Your School Achieving Excellence and Equity?

This self-assessment will help you establish a data profile with evidence of progress toward excellence and equity. Consider working with a team of educators to examine and compile these data. Think broadly about performance data collected and reported by your state, including promotion rates, graduation rates, proficiency rates, attendance rates, enrollment in special programs, performance on college entrance exams, etc. Completion of the self-assessment will generate a picture of the school's current performance. By utilizing the same process annually or semi-annually, the school can assess progress toward excellence and equity for all student groups. NOTE: Wherever the words "the average of all students in your state" appear, it is important to note that you are encouraged to compare the performance of the particular group addressed at your school with the performance of all *students in your state (not simply the comparable population in your state).*

I. Racial/Ethnic Groups

    A. Which major racial/ethnic groups are served at your school? (List every group with more than 20 students.)

    B. For each racial/ethnic group listed, what data suggest that the students from the group perform above or below the average of all students in your state?

    C. What data suggest that the students from the group are demonstrating improved academic performance at a rate that is greater or less than the overall rate of improvement for students in your state?

II. Language Background Group

    A. Which major language background groups are served at your school? (List every language that represents the language background of at least 20 students.)

    B. For each language background listed, what data suggest that the students from the group perform above or below the average of all students in your state?

    C. What data suggest that the students from each language group are demonstrating improved academic performances at a rate that is greater or less than the overall rate of improvement for students in your state?

    D. What data suggest that the students from each language group are achieving mastery of English at a rate that exceeds other students in your state?

    E. What data suggest that students from each language group are developing, maintaining, and strengthening mastery of their native language?

III. Low-Income Groups

    A. What data suggest that students who meet low-income criteria are performing above or below the average of all students in your state?

    B. What data suggest that students who meet low-income criteria are demonstrating improved academic performances at a rate that is greater or less than the overall rate of improvement for students in your state?

C. Which special low-income groups does your school serve? (e.g., students experiencing homelessness, foster children)

D. What data suggest that these special low-income groups are performing above or below the average of all students in your state?

E. What data suggest that these special low-income groups are demonstrating improved academic performances at a rate that is greater or less than the overall rate of improvement for students in your state?

IV. Gender and Gender-Related Groups

A. What data suggest that males and females are performing above or below the average for all students in your state?

B. What data suggest that males and females are demonstrating improved academic performances at a rate that is greater or less than the overall rate of improvement for students in your state?

C. Which gender-related groups (e.g., transgender students) are served at your school?

D. What data suggest that each gender-related group is performing above or below the average for all students in your state?

E. What data suggest that each gender-related group is demonstrating improved academic performances at a rate that is greater or less than the overall rate of improvement for students in your state?

V. Geographic Groups

A. Which major groups of students at your school are identifiable based upon the location of their homes? (e.g., students who live in different neighborhoods, a major apartment complex, a gated community)

B. What data suggest that students in each geographic area are performing above or below the average for all students in your state?

C. What data suggest that students in each geographic area are demonstrating improved academic performances at a rate that is greater or less than the overall rate of improvement for students in your state?

VI. Group Intersections

A. Which groups of students, defined by the intersections of two or more groups listed above, might be performing at levels that are substantially different from the levels of performances of any of the groups that comprise the intersection? (For example, do Black male students at your school perform at substantially different levels than either Black students or male students at your school?)

B. What data suggest that students in each intersection group identified above (VI. A.) are performing above or below the average for all students in your state?

C. What data suggest that students in each intersection group are demonstrating improved academic performances at a rate that is greater or less than the overall rate of improvement for students in your state?

References

Bogotch, I. E. (2002). Educational leadership and social justice: Practice into theory. *Journal of School Leadership, 12*, 138–156.

Brookover, W. B., & Lezotte, L. W. (1979). *Changes in school characteristics coincident with changes in student achievement.* Occasional paper No. 17 (ED181005).

Brookover, W. B., & Schneider, J. M. (1975). Academic environments and elementary school achievement. *Journal of Research and Development in Education, 9*, 82–91.

Carr, S. (July–August 2008). Editor's notebook: A quotation with a life of its own. *Patient Safety and Quality Healthcare.* Retrieved from http://psqh.com/editor-s-notebook-a-quotation-with-a-life-of-its-own.

Coleman, J. S., Campbell, E. Q., Hobson, C. J., McPartland, J., Mood, A.M., Weinfeld, F. D., & York, R. L. (1966). *Equality of educational opportunities.* Washington, DC: U.S. Office of Education (ED 012 275).

Dantley, M., & Tillman, L. (2006). Social justice and moral transformative leadership. In C. Marshall & M. Olivia (Eds.), *Leadership for social justice: Making revolutions happen* (pp. 16–29). Boston, MA: Pearson.

DeMatthews, D. (2015). Making sense of social justice leadership: A case study of a principal's experiences to create a more inclusive school. *Leadership and Policy in Schools, 14*(2), 139–166, DOI: 10.1080/15700763.2014.997939.

Edmonds, R. (1979). Effective schools for the urban poor. *Educational Leadership, 37*(1), 15–18, 20–24.

Furman, G. (2012). Social justice leadership as praxis: Developing capacities through preparation programs. *Educational Administration Quarterly, 48*, 191–229.

Jean-Marie, G. (2008). Leadership for social justice: An agenda for 21st century schools. *Educational Forum, 72*, 340–354.

Lightfoot, S. L. (1981). Portraits of exemplary secondary schools: George Washington Carver Comprehensive High School. *Daedalus, 110*(4), 17–37.

Marshall, C., & Ward, M. (2004). "Yes, but . . .": Education leaders discuss social justice. *Journal of School Leadership, 14*, 530–563.

Scheurich, J., & Skrla, L. (2003). *Leadership for equity and excellence: Creating high achievement classrooms, schools, and districts.* Thousand Oaks, CA: Corwin Press, Inc.

Theoharis, G. (2007). Social justice educational leaders and resistance: Toward a theory of social justice leadership. *Educational Administration Quarterly, 43*(2), 221–258.

Theoharis, G. (2009). *School leaders our children deserve: Seven keys to equity, social justice, and school reform*. New York: Teachers College Press.

Venezky, R.L., & Winfield, L.F. (1979). *Schools that succeed beyond expectations in reading* (Studies on Education Technical Report No. 1). Newark: University of Delaware (ERIC Document Reproduction Service No. ED 177 484).

Weber, G. (1971). *Inner-city children can be taught to read: Four successful schools*. Washington, DC: Council for Basic Education.

Positive Transformational Culture

2

When a kid walks through this door, the principal feels like that's her child. Every single one of us feels that way . . . That's the caring that is in this building. Some of these kids don't get any of this love at home. Homework will go, and it may not come back. And we have people here who will say, "Sit over here and let's do this work" or "Go over there to Ms. So-and-so who is going to 'adopt' you, and she is going to help you with this work." That's how we care here.

Teacher, R. N. Harris Elementary, Durham, NC

Our most consistent finding about high-performing urban schools is that they established a positive, transformational culture that made the school a place where all students (regardless of race/ethnicity, family income, language background, gender, sexual orientation, disability status, or other demographic group) were eager to come to school, learn, and grow. As well, the school became a place where adults (teachers, support staff, volunteers, and administrators) were eager to come to work, learn, and grow as members of a team that made an increasingly powerful difference in the lives of students. A school's culture comprises the beliefs and values of its members (Schein, 1992) and is reflected in norms and traditions formed over time (Deal & Peterson, 2009). School culture guides behavior according to underlying assumptions that are shared by teachers, reflected in administrators, students, parents, support personnel, and others (Schein, 1992).

We define the culture as *positive*, because these high-performing urban schools displayed overwhelmingly positive learning climates for all these stakeholders. Children and adults felt respected, valued, and appreciated. Adults took painstaking efforts to ensure that everyone felt safe and comfortable (physically and emotionally).

Students perceived that the adults at school knew them and cared about them individually. School employees perceived that administrators wanted them to be professionally successful. There was little evidence of personal tension among students, among adults, or between students and adults. Rare incidents of student misbehavior were handled in a low-key manner that helped sustain the positive climate. In elementary, middle, and high schools, we observed comfortable classroom atmospheres with minimal tension between teachers and students and minimal tension among students. "There isn't much drama here," one student from Dayton Business Technology High School explained. She emphasized, "People get along and help each other."

Students wanted to come to school and learn not only because adults created a pleasant, safe environment, but also because adults convinced students that the entire school community was committed to their success. In many of the awarded schools, students told interviewers, "The teachers here care about us. They want us to succeed." At Maplewood Richmond Heights High School near St. Louis, a student explained, "They [teachers] know we can do college-level work and they won't rest and they won't let us rest until we do it." Ladson-Billings (2002) emphasized that caring educators demanded that students work hard to succeed. Irvine and Fraser (1998) described educators who exhibited this style of caring as "warm demanders." Bondy and Ross (2008) reported that warm demanders knew their students as individuals, demonstrated unconditional positive regard, and then insisted that students perform to high standards. Warm demanders dominated the cultures of these high-performing urban schools.

The culture was *transformational* because students, teachers, support personnel, and administrators were always focused on improving. Even when the school had achieved at levels far beyond typical expectations for urban schools, teachers were asking, "How can I improve that lesson so that more students will understand the central concepts?" Teachers were willing to modify their instructional strategies, homework assignments, lesson plans, and daily routines in order to generate better learning results for students. Counselors were constantly analyzing data and asking how they might intervene in ways that better helped students adjust to difficult life situations. Administrators were constantly considering how they might help teachers effectively reach more students. Administrators were willing to modify master schedules, professional development calendars, program budgets, discipline policies, job descriptions, and almost anything else they controlled or influenced if it was likely to result in greater successes for all students.

In these schools, the sense of hope promoted an even greater collective commitment to transformation. Hope influenced the extent to which students, parents, teachers, and other school personnel sought to improve their efforts. Educators nurtured a sense of hope by helping students and parents envision a better future. Conversations about college and careers occurred frequently at these schools. Students learned to see themselves as changing the trajectory of their lives and changing the future of their communities. As well, school personnel recognized that working as a team provided a real opportunity to change the lives of students and families.

Educators were constantly focused on ensuring the success of each and every student. "We're not necessarily sure about how we will make it happen," explained one teacher at Dandy Middle School in Fort Lauderdale, Florida, "but, we're not giving up until we get every student to a place where we know they will do well in high school." While educators recognized the tremendous barriers they faced related to poverty, family traumas, racial issues, neighborhood violence, and a multitude of other concerns, they continued to assume that they could transform their schools into places where all children (from every demographic group) could excel, as measured by whichever variables they deemed important.

Educators expected themselves to lead students to understand challenging concepts and master complicated skills. In spite of challenges associated with their students' low family incomes, prior lack of quality schooling, lack of mastery of academic English, or need for a vast array of social services, they chose to assume that they could plan together, implement strategies, examine learning results, and make smart refinements that would ultimately result in the success of each and every student at their school.

Educators exhibited a sense of urgency to shape programs, policies, and practices in ways that would lead each and every student to success. When teachers presented lessons, they wanted to know if students mastered the objectives taught. If they saw evidence that some students or groups of students did not demonstrate mastery, they wanted to know how they could make the lesson more effective. If all students demonstrated mastery, the teachers challenged themselves to consider what specific practices they might replicate and apply to other learning objectives so that students might experience additional successes. When teachers saw that a colleague's students achieved great learning results, they did not respond with angst, skepticism, or jealousy, seeking reasons to discredit their colleague. Instead, they aimed to learn about the strategies, approaches, or techniques the colleague used that they might apply to help their own students achieve mastery.

For example, at Highland Elementary School in Silver Spring, Maryland, when one teacher succeeded in helping almost all of her English learners to master a challenging literacy concept, the other teachers attentively took notes as the teacher explained the strategies she used to make concepts clear and familiar to her students. The culture of the school was such that academic successes were valued as professional learning opportunities.

While educators demanded much of themselves, they also provided each other with a high level of support. Often, interviewers heard teachers report, "We're like a family here." One teacher at Escontrias Elementary in El Paso, Texas explained, "We rally around each other. We try to help each other so that we can all be strong teachers. We're OK as individuals, but as a team, we're pretty amazing."

Positive Transformational Culture as the Foundation

In these schools, curricular and instructional strength were built upon a foundational culture that helped teachers, students, parents, and support personnel feel valued and appreciated.

The positive transformational culture influenced every aspect of schooling: student behavior, classroom instruction, extra-curricular activities, professional learning communities, professional development, school routines, procedures, policies, and more. As well, the positive transformational culture influenced changes that improved learning results for every racial/ethnic group, every language group, students with disabilities, and other groups of students who had typically not excelled at school. Educators did not simply seek to transform the schooling experience for one demographic group of students. Instead, they sought to ensure success for every group they served. As a result, students perceived that their success in school was likely. The positive transformational culture made school a place where all demographic groups of students wanted to learn and grow.

As discussed in Chapter 1, each of the empowering school characteristics, including challenging curricula, effective instruction, and a positive, transformational culture, played a central role in the success of the high-performing schools we awarded and studied. All three supported the pursuit of excellence and equity; however, these three distinguishing characteristics did not carry equal weight. Instead, our conceptualization of these influencing features of school life looks more like Figure 2.1, in which positive transformational culture serves as a foundation for efforts to improve curriculum and instruction. In these schools, curricular and instructional strength were built upon a foundational culture that helped teachers, students, parents, and support personnel feel valued and appreciated. Fisher, Frey, and Pumpian (2012) expressed this concept by writing about the relationship between academic press and school culture. They explained, "Academic press is absolutely necessary, but not sufficient to operationalize the mission of the school. We believe that no school improvement effort will be effective, maintained, or enhanced unless school culture and academic press are both addressed and aligned" (Fisher et al., 2012, p. 5). In the high-performing schools we studied, it is unlikely that individuals would have invested the necessary energy to pursue curricular and instructional transformations, in the absence of a culture that made them feel like they belonged as part of a larger family system.

Figure 2.1. School Characteristics that Empowered the Pursuit of Excellence and Equity

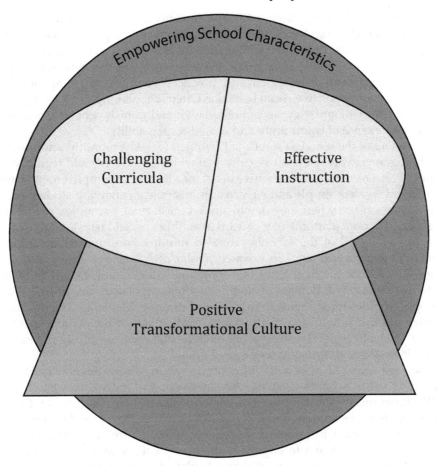

The Power of a Coherent Educational Improvement System to Create and Sustain Positive Transformational Cultures

Neumerski (2013) noted that many schools and districts struggle to generate improved achievement for their urban students, in part, because their schools lack collectively constructed, specific, stable, and aligned instructional systems. Without coherent educational improvement systems, urban schools and districts look for heroic teachers and charismatic principals to lift them beyond minimal academic expectations.

In the high-performing urban schools we studied, positive transformational cultures did not develop by chance. Leaders conceptualized and nurtured a strong, coherent educational improvement system that played a critical role in initiating, developing, and sustaining these cultures. In fact, one could say, these schools were "perfectly designed" to create positive transformational cultures.

Leading Stakeholders to Feel Valued and Capable

As part of a coherent system, educators in many of the high-performing urban schools developed or implemented programs for creating a positive learning environment for students. Programs like Positive Behavioral Intervention and Support (PBIS) played a major role in shaping the interactions of teachers and students. Teachers and students established and practiced routines that emphasized the acknowledgment of positive social behavior. Often schools employed strategies that were intended to minimize cycles of misbehavior and punishment and instead promote a deeper sense of community and shared responsibility.

Almost all of the schools established frequent (weekly, monthly, and quarterly) award programs to build a positive culture in which all students had regular opportunities to earn recognition for positive behavior, effort, or accomplishment. Some of these programs were simple and easy to administer (e.g., allowing students to visit the principal's office when they demonstrated mastery of a complex concept) and some required more planning (e.g., award assemblies or field trips).

Additionally, all of the schools provided multiple, positive opportunities for students to engage and excel in extra-curricular activities. System elements were designed to reduce the likelihood that individual students or groups of students would feel disengaged. Before-, during-, and after-school activities provided abundant opportunities for students to explore and develop talents, experience success, and earn positive recognition. For instance, at West Manor Elementary in Atlanta, Georgia, students enjoyed a wide array of clubs that focus on hip-hop dance, gardening, journalism, technology, tennis, and drama.

Even the sense of hope was influenced systematically. Several of the high-performing urban schools used the Advancement Via Individual Determination (AVID) Program, or similar program components, to help students and parents understand how the student could realistically pursue, attend, and succeed in college. Schools worked to establish a "college-going culture" and provided many opportunities for students to engage with current college students or recent college graduates. All of these system elements played important roles in helping the schools become more positive places for students.

In many cases, the school buildings themselves reinforced the positive culture. Certain building conditions and design features (cleanliness, ease of movement, aesthetic appeal, an abundance of natural light, flexible and responsive classrooms, sufficient room for learning and exploration, and safety and security) help to foster a sense of belonging, a sense of control and competence, and a sense of collective commitment to a school and its purposes (Uline, Tschannen-Moran, & Wolsey, 2009; Uline et al., 2010). In a number of the high-performing schools studied, we observed the way flexible and responsive learning environments created a sense of comfort, inviting students to move within and beyond their individual classrooms. Leaders at Revere High School in Revere, Massachusetts initiated a renovation of the school library, creating a college-like setting with an abundance of technology, comfortable furniture, and open spaces where students could gather to engage actively in their own, and each other's, learning. Specific structural and furniture arrangements also impacted the quantity and quality of the professional relationships between teachers. At James Pace Early College High School in Brownsville, Texas, the war room provided a large, comfortable space where teachers collaborated frequently amidst carefully organized displays of current student data.

Colors, shapes, textures, and unique features of these schools added to the overall aesthetic, creating a sense of affinity to the school as a positive place of learning. The campus of National City Middle School in Southern California's Sweetwater Union High School District comprised a number of new facilities, along with older buildings in need of repair. The school custodian described the ways in which he and his staff went the extra mile to make these older structures more inviting places for students, school personnel, and the community.

> When I first came, the older buildings were all brown. Somebody came with the paint, maybe it was on sale, and painted *everything* brown. One of our custodians repainted each and every one of the older buildings, featuring the school's colors, off-white with blue and yellow trim. He came before his 2:30 shift and donated three hours of his time each day until the job was finished.

Although many of the high-performing schools we studied were not new or state of the art, they did stand as places of pride for their occupants and their communities. Renovations to Maplewood Richmond Heights High School near St. Louis transformed the building into a learning environment more reminiscent of a private prep school than an aging and inadequate urban high school. The resulting improvements exposed existing fireplaces, refurbished stately, built-in bookshelves, and restored beautiful oak millwork throughout the building. From small study alcoves to state-of-the-art music facilities, learning spaces generated a pride of place that served the educational mission of the school, strengthening the connections between students, school personnel, and community stakeholders.

Consistent with efforts to make students feel valued and capable, schools developed structures, routines, policies, and norms to build the connection between teachers and families. For example, at MacArthur Senior High School in Houston's Aldine Independent School District, teachers rode school buses into their students' neighborhoods so they could learn more about where students lived and the daily challenges students and families faced. It was also common for teachers and administrators to greet parents and students as parents dropped off their children in the morning. Parents at Signal Hill Elementary in Long Beach claimed, "The principal makes you feel like a hero just because you got your child to school on time." Many schools promoted regular opportunities for students, parents, and teachers to interact and get to know each other. In several of the schools, teachers made regular positive phone calls to parents. As a parent of a middle school student from KIPP Adelante in San Diego explained:

> When I looked at my phone and saw that the school was calling, I thought, "What did my Rogelio do now?" But then, it was the teacher. And she was explaining how my Rogelio was participating in class each day and how he had done all his homework. And, I wondered, "Is she talking about my Rogelio?" But, she was. And then, a few weeks later she called again with another good report about my son.

Systematic efforts to call parents and share positive news built stronger relationships between teachers and parents. Parents perceived greater hope for their children's academic success. Additionally, parents were more likely to respond positively when teachers called with requests or concerns.

In addition to building relationships with parents, educators in high-performing urban schools systematically built the capacity of parents to help transform the school. For example, at Granger Junior High in the Sweetwater Union High School District near San Diego, school leaders trained parents to know what they should look for when they visited their children's classrooms. At many of the high-performing schools (e.g., Escontrias Elementary in El Paso's Socorro Independent School District), teachers held special English classes for parents. In many schools, like Lauderbach and Otay Elementary Schools in Chula Vista, California, teachers sent home daily checklists to keep parents abreast of their children's progress and to facilitate stronger parent/school communication and collaboration.

In a similar way, the high-performing schools utilized collaborative teams as part of a coherent system for creating positive environments for educators. Not all of the schools called their collaborative teams "PLCs"; however, almost all of the schools employed systems designed to work like PLCs (DuFour & Marzano, 2011). The collaborative teams met regularly (in many schools they met once a week or even more frequently). The meetings provided the participants with a true sense of community, characterized by a high level of trust and a commitment to each other's personal and professional success. Teachers were far less likely to feel isolated or disconnected than teachers in more typical schools. In contrast, teachers were more likely to feel like they were part of a strong, professional team.

Leading Educators to Develop a Focus on Teaching a Set of Important, Challenging Concepts and Skills

As educators developed a focus on important, challenging concepts and skills, they helped students perceive that they were valued and capable. Students from many of the high-performing schools expressed pride in the challenging concepts and skills they were learning in school. For example, a student at Golden Empire Elementary in Sacramento, California exclaimed, "I'm in fourth grade and I'm learning stuff in science that my brother is learning. And, he's in middle school!" Similarly, a student at Cecil H. Parker Elementary in Mount Vernon, New York explained,

"At my other school, they only gave us baby work. Here, they expect us to learn *real* math." The structures that helped teachers set specific, challenging academic learning targets also helped students perceive that they were academically and intellectually capable.

The impact of collective efforts to establish challenging learning targets was intensified as teachers used various routines to share the learning targets with students and parents. At several schools, the weekly focus standards or key learning targets or MIOs (Most Important Objectives) were discussed in classes, disseminated in newsletters to parents, described on classroom learning management system pages, or displayed prominently on classroom walls. Students talked eagerly about what they were learning and accomplishing. Parents expressed pride in their children's abilities. The open discussion of the challenging academic standards students were learning deepened students' confidence about their ability to succeed academically.

Leading Educators to Improve the Effectiveness of Initial Instruction

Systematic efforts to improve the quality of initial instruction also influenced the development of a transformational culture for educators in the high-performing urban schools studied. In particular, collaborative teams created a safe environment for teachers to learn, ask questions, try new strategies, and support each other as they worked to increase levels of mastery. In several of the schools, teachers reported that their PLCs met more frequently than the principal required. For example, a teacher at Highland Elementary in Montgomery County, Maryland explained:

> At first we met because we had to meet. Now, we meet because we fuel each other. We help each other think, plan, and grow. I can't imagine teaching without my team. If we're not teaching, we're usually meeting to plan our teaching.

Collaborative teams helped develop a positive climate for educators, and they also helped develop a commitment to transforming teaching and learning. Consistently and frequently, teachers engaged in discussions that were grounded in a commitment to improving the quality of teaching and learning in each teacher's classroom. Educators openly, carefully, and thoughtfully examined their students' work in a way that maximized their own learning about practices that were more likely to lead their students to high levels of mastery. Through collaborative teams, educators came to recognize their power to transform learning environments in ways that resulted in better learning results for all their students.

School leaders played a vital role in providing and protecting sufficient time for teachers to meet as collaborative teams. As well, leaders provided necessary resources to support the ongoing inquiry that is central to the work of PLCs (Louis, Marks, & Kruse, 1996; Mullen & Hutinger, 2008; Olivier & Hipp, 2006). In fact, in these high-performing urban schools, school leaders frequently participated in the meetings, providing direction, offering support, and monitoring the tone of meetings to ensure that trust was developed and nurtured and to ensure that each meeting helped teachers build upon their strengths. In his book *Visible learning*, Hattie reminds us, "It is school leaders who promote challenging goals, and then establish safe environments for teachers to critique, question and support other teachers to reach these goals together that have the most effect on student outcomes" (2009, pp. 83–84).

School leaders engaged in other systems-focused behavior that influenced the development of a positive transformational culture (while simultaneously improving instruction). In particular, school leaders in high-performing urban schools spent far more time observing classroom instruction and providing constructive feedback than did principals in more typical schools. In fact, a growing body of research bears this out. In earlier comparison studies, the principals of exceptionally high-achieving schools differed from their counterparts in consistently low-achieving schools in the amount of time spent directly observing classroom practices and facilitating instruction-related discussions (Heck, 1992). Similarly, across 27 studies analyzed by Robinson and colleagues (2008), research involving such between-group comparisons found substantial differences in the leadership of otherwise similar high- and low-performing schools. Teachers in high-performing schools reported that their principals served as a valuable instructional resource, actively participating in their learning and development.

Often teachers in the high-performing schools reported that they were accustomed to seeing principals and assistant principals in their classrooms weekly or even more frequently. Frequently, principals had routines that ensured that they dedicated time each day for visiting classrooms. A teacher at Horace Mann Elementary in Glendale, CA exclaimed, "If the principal hasn't been in my classroom for a day or two, I want to find out what's wrong!"

Teachers spoke positively about the frequent classroom observations they received from their administrators. This is likely due to their perception that observations were not high-stakes events. In contrast, teachers perceived that their administrators were present because they cared about each teacher's success. Teachers perceived that administrators offered useful assistance that helped them better meet the needs of the diverse learners they served.

Through their classroom observations and feedback, leaders demonstrated their willingness to support teachers. In high-performing schools, leaders contributed to the establishment of a trusting, supportive environment by being present to notice the accomplishments of teachers and students, reinforcing even small improvements in teaching and learning, and offering support that helped teachers accomplish their goals for student success. Often leaders incorporated these kinds of supports into their routines by writing and leaving brief notes, sending short congratulatory email messages, or intentionally acknowledging teacher/classroom accomplishments during faculty meetings or professional development sessions.

In addition to creating a more positive learning climate for teachers, classroom observations influenced the positive climate for students. Johnson, Uline, and Perez (2011) noted that leaders in high-performing urban schools paid particular attention to the classroom climate for students. Frequently, observations and feedback helped teachers create classroom environments that were caring, nurturing, and welcoming. By looking for and providing feedback related to relational issues, principals increased the likelihood that every teacher provided a supportive, positive classroom climate. One principal justified this focus by explaining, "If the teacher has solid relationships that are caring and nurturing, students will succeed."

Leading Educators to Improve the Effectiveness of Intervention and Enrichment

In high-performing urban schools, fewer students require intervention because the initial instruction provided by teachers is more likely to lead students to mastery. Nonetheless, at these schools we noted a strong commitment to structures and routines that helped students achieve mastery when initial instruction was not successful. As well, educators were likely to return to concepts and push for greater application, deeper analysis, or more detailed understanding even when students achieved initial mastery. While every one of the high-performing schools studied exceeded district and state achievement expectations, the schools continued to strive to improve learning results. The transformational aspect of the school culture was strongly influenced by school-wide structures and routines.

Teacher collaboration was a major engine in the thrust for continuous improvement. In collaborative teams, teachers continued to scrutinize student work and look for opportunities to improve and extend instructional strategies. Their analysis of student work was not simply for the purpose of grading. Teacher teams were committed to understanding how they could help more students achieve mastery. They sought to refine lesson designs in ways that maximized student engagement and minimized students' misconceptions. Even when students answered correctly, teachers asked, "But, do they know why this is correct?" And, they designed enrichment activities to help students acquire deeper understandings of key concepts.

Cycles of classroom observation and feedback also influenced the transformational culture of the schools. Even when achievement results exceeded district and state expectations, administrators continued to spend substantial amounts of time visiting classrooms and providing feedback designed to help teachers build upon their instructional strengths and address opportunities for improvement. Administrators gave special attention to the practices their teachers implemented that were proving influential. By acknowledging successes, leaders helped all teachers implement effective intervention and enrichment strategies to further improve learning results. Even as the schools achieved important local, state, and national recognition, educators continued to strive to reach more students and deepen student understanding. An ethic of continuous improvement compelled everyone to examine learning results, celebrate accomplishments, refine approaches, and strive for even greater results for every demographic group served.

Summary

While educators in the high-performing schools confronted the everyday realities of urban communities, they exuded a positive belief in their collective capacity to transform the schooling experiences of students.

Positive transformational cultures provided the foundation that helped schools achieve excellent and equitable learning results. The school culture positively influenced students' desire to attend school, work hard, and excel. As well, the culture positively influenced adults' commitment to engage, work hard, and help their students and their colleagues excel. The culture promoted an urgency to improve (even when the results achieved already exceeded the expectations of others external to the school). The culture emphasized and promoted improvement for every demographic group served and every individual student.

Specifically, the positive transformational culture resulted in the following:

♦ Students from all demographic groups indicated they were convinced that the adults at the school knew them and cared about them, their present situations, and their future successes.

♦ Students from all demographic groups perceived that instruction was interesting and engaging. Students perceived that their teachers worked hard to create lessons that related to their interests, backgrounds, and cultures. Students felt stimulated and challenged intellectually, without feeling overwhelmed.

♦ Students from all demographic groups received considerable positive attention from teachers and classmates because of the positive, constructive things they did. Students did not need to engage in negative behavior in order to attract attention.

♦ Students from all demographic groups experienced multiple avenues for achieving success and recognition. Educators (often working alongside community members and parents) developed curricular and extra-curricular opportunities for students to experience meaningful success. Often, every student interviewed could identify an activity, subject, or area of performance in which the student felt a sense of accomplishment and pride. Because of the positive feedback provided by educators, students felt hopeful about their academic future.

♦ Students perceived that adult expectations were clear, reasonable, and consistent. Rules and expectations were not overly restrictive. Students from all demographic groups felt like they could "be themselves" without breaking the rules. Students felt like they belonged at their school.

♦ Students from all demographic groups perceived that adults at the school wanted them (the students) at school every day, valued their presence, and respected them (not because of the implications for school funding, but because of the unique value of each student).

♦ When students needed to be redirected, teachers did so in a low-key manner. Minimal attention was given to misbehavior. Teachers were very respectful of students from all demographic groups and took care to avoid embarrassing them.

♦ Students from all demographic groups reported that they felt safe at school and in their classrooms. They believed that the adults at school would keep them safe from physical, emotional, or psychological harm.

♦ Proactively, adults addressed potentially challenging situations in ways that prevented academic and/or social problems. Often adults at the school established positive connections with students' parents or guardians before issues emerged.

♦ Students from all demographic groups felt empowered to nurture their own academic, social, and personal growth.

♦ Students from all demographic groups perceived that the educators cared enough about them to change routines, procedures, materials, strategies, practices, and policies in order to ensure their success.

Also, the positive transformational culture made school a place where educators were eager to come to work, learn, and grow, and be part of a team that made an increasingly powerful difference in the lives of students. Specifically, the positive transformational culture resulted in the following:

♦ Educators believed that their students had the capacity to achieve at high levels and master challenging academic curricula. Relatedly, educators believed that, as a team, they had the capacity to ensure that their students achieved at high levels.

♦ Educators believed that they were working toward important life-changing outcomes for their students. They believed they were doing more than achieving bureaucratic benchmarks, raising test scores, or complying with federal, state, or district expectations.

♦ Educators believed that administrators and school leaders cared deeply about students.

♦ Educators believed that administrators and school leaders knew them and cared deeply about them and their colleagues (personally and professionally).

♦ Educators perceived that they were working in collaboration with a powerful professional team. They belonged to the team. They perceived that the team was strong enough to successfully influence meaningful changes in the lives of the diverse groups of students the school served.

♦ Educators perceived that the expectations articulated by their administrators and school leaders were clear, reasonable, and consistent. Educators knew what leaders looked for and expected. Educators believed that their leaders' expectations were challenging, but necessary for the school's success.

♦ Educators perceived that collaborative efforts at their school were both abundant and professionally valuable. Educators reported that they were more successful in responding to the needs of their diverse groups of students because of the high-quality collaborative efforts in which they participated.

♦ Educators believed that their colleagues perceived them as important contributors to the school's transformational efforts. Educators believed that their colleagues recognized and valued their contributions, especially those contributions that resulted in measurable gains for the diverse groups of students who traditionally had not achieved academic success.

♦ Educators from all demographic groups reported that they felt physically and emotionally safe at school and in their classrooms.

♦ Educators perceived that their administrators and school leaders were much more interested in helping them than punishing them. They perceived that school leaders held high expectations for educators. They also perceived that school leaders had great capacity to help educators meet those high expectations.

♦ Educators felt empowered to nurture their own pedagogical, academic, social, and personal growth.

Beyond affirming each stakeholder's value, the positive culture led stakeholders to value ongoing transformation. Students and adults perceived both an opportunity and a mandate to participate in rethinking and reshaping programs, policies, and practices in ways that led to excellent and equitable learning results. While educators in the high-performing schools confronted the everyday realities of urban communities, they exuded a positive belief in their collective capacity to transform the schooling experiences of students. The excitement generated by improved results fueled the expectation that even greater results could be achieved.

What It Is & What It Isn't: Positive Transformational Culture

What It Is: Environment of Trust and Mutual Respect

Educators interact in an environment of trust and mutual respect where each individual is constantly trying to improve outcomes for students. Regularly, educators invite each other (and their administrators) into their classrooms. They share ideas and support each other in generating better learning results for students. Teachers believe that administrators and colleagues are eager to support them (personally and professionally). Educators feel like they are part of an amazing team that is constantly improving results for students.

What It Isn't: Environment of Suspicion and Fear

Administrators insist that educators collaborate; however, teachers aren't sure why. Many suspect the real goal is to shame lower performing teachers into leaving. Teachers are reluctant to share instructional problems, because they don't know how the information will be used. While there are school mission statements that emphasize teamwork, teachers often feel an allegiance to "teams" that work against each other.

* * *

What It Is: Students Feel Valued, Respected, and Loved

Students feel personally valued, respected, and loved. They report that teachers care about them individually and they cite a wide range of evidence (e.g., the posting of excellent student work, the effort exerted to create engaging lessons, the personalized greetings teachers extend to students, the school-wide efforts to create physically and emotionally safe learning environments, the strategies teachers use to elicit student engagement). Students are comfortable taking academic/intellectual risks because they are confident that their teachers care deeply about their growth and learning.

What It Isn't: Students Feel Controlled

Students behave well, but typically do not engage with their teachers or with each other. Students follow rigid rules, because they fear the consequences for misbehavior. Students are reluctant to guess incorrectly or take risks. Teachers report that they care about their students; however, students think that teachers care about them only when they perform well academically and follow the rules. Some teachers and administrators fear their students, especially larger, older males of color. Fear influences the extent to which some teachers exclude students covertly (by ignoring them) or overtly (by removing them from the classroom or from the school).

*   *   *

What It Is: Educators Believe in Their Students

Even though school personnel acknowledge the financial, social, and academic challenges faced by many of their students, they eagerly point to the many accomplishments of their students as evidence of potential. Educators express a sincere optimism about their students' capacity to succeed at high levels. As well, educators are optimistic about their capacity to influence their students' success. Educators are determined to find ways to help every student excel.

What It Isn't: Educators Are Convinced that Nothing More Can Be Done

School personnel appear overwhelmed by the financial, social, and academic challenges faced by many of their students. They want the best for their students, but they have difficulty seeing how most students could escape the negative impacts of their home situations. Teachers believe that they already do the best that can be done, considering the challenges their students face at home, in the community, or in the classroom.

*   *   *

What It Is: Educators Show Positive Regard for Parents and Families

School personnel display a sincere respect for the parents and families of their students. School personnel have taken the time to meet and get to know many of the families they serve. Educators try to adapt programs, policies, and procedures in ways that maximize parent engagement. Educators find ways to minimize the impact of language differences (and other differences) and make parents feel comfortable. Parents are convinced that the teachers and administrators want their children to succeed at school and in life.

What It Isn't: Educators Don't Know the Parents or Families of Their Students

Educators have minimal contact with the parents of their students. Typically, contact occurs only when educators must notify parents about student problems. Teachers assume that most parents do not care about their children's success at school. Teachers assume that communication with families would be difficult or impossible because of language barriers, cultural differences, or differences in values.

School Self-Assessment Tool: Does Your School Have a Positive Transformational Culture?

This self-assessment will help you determine the extent to which your school has a positive transformational culture. Consider working with a team of teachers, administrators, parents, and students to respond to these questions. (One could invite participants to provide individual ratings.) Completion of the self-assessment will generate a picture of the school's current culture. By utilizing the same process annually or semi-annually, the school can assess progress toward developing a positive transformational culture.

I. List all major demographic groups served at your school. For each group listed, rate the following on a scale of 1 to 5, with 1 representing NOT LIKELY and 5 representing VERY LIKELY:

a. To what extent are students in the group likely to perceive that adults at the school know them personally? Rating: _____

b. To what extent are students in the group likely to perceive that adults at the school care about their current and future academic success? Rating: _____

c. To what extent are students in the group likely to perceive that they are physically and emotionally safe when they are at school? Rating: _____

d. To what extent are students in the group likely to perceive that they have multiple, realistic opportunities to achieve positive recognition related to their character or their academic or non-academic accomplishments? Rating: _____

e. To what extent are students in the group likely to perceive that adults enjoy seeing them at school? Rating: _____

f. To what extent are students in the group likely to perceive that they have a strong chance to graduate from high school? Rating: _____

g. To what extent are students in the group likely to perceive that they have a strong chance to attend and succeed in college? Rating: _____

h. To what extent are students in the group likely to work diligently to learn whatever concepts or skills their teachers endeavor to teach? Rating: _____

II. For school personnel at your school, rate the following on a scale of 1 to 5, with 1 representing NOT LIKELY and 5 representing VERY LIKELY:

    a. To what extent are school personnel likely to perceive that other adults at the school know them personally? Rating: _____

    b. To what extent are school personnel likely to perceive that their peers at the school care about their current and future professional success? Rating: _____

    c. To what extent are school personnel likely to perceive that school leaders care about their current and future professional success? Rating: _____

    d. To what extent are school personnel likely to perceive that they are physically and emotionally safe when they are at school? Rating:

_____

    e. To what extent are school personnel likely to perceive that their efforts to improve their performance will be noticed and appreciated? Rating: _____

    f. To what extent are school personnel likely to perceive that their peers enjoy seeing them at school? Rating: _____

    g. To what extent are school personnel likely to perceive that they are a valued part of a team that is making a positive difference for students? Rating: _____

    h. To what extent are school personnel continuously assessing the impact of their work on students in the school? Rating: _____

    i. To what extent are school personnel likely to work diligently to improve their performance in ways that lead to better outcomes for students? Rating: _____

    j. To what extent do school personnel challenge and support each other to improve outcomes for students continuously? Rating: _____

References

Bondy, E., & Ross, D.D. (2008). The teacher as warm demander. *Educational Leadership, 66*(1), 54–58.

Deal, T.E., & Peterson, K.D. (2009). *Shaping school culture: Pitfalls, paradoxes, and promises*, 2nd ed. San Francisco, CA: John Wiley & Sons, Inc.

Dufour, R., & Marzano, R.J. (2011). *Leaders of learning: How district, school, and classroom leaders improve student achievement*. Bloomington, IN: Solution Tree Press.

Fisher, D., Frey, N., & Pumpian, I. (2012). *How to create a culture of achievement in your school and classroom*. Alexandria, VA: Association for Supervision and Curriculum Development.

Hattie, J. (2009). *Visible learning: A synthesis of over 800 meta-analyses relating to achievement*. London: Routledge.

Heck, R. (1992). Principals' instructional leadership and school performance: Implications for policy development. *Educational Evaluation of Policy Analysis, 14*(1), 21–34.

Irvine, J. J., & Fraser, J. W. (1998). Warm demanders. *Education Week, 17*(35), 56.

Johnson, J. F., Uline, C. L., & Perez, L. G. (2011). Expert noticing and principals of high-performing urban schools. *Journal of Education for Students Placed at Risk, 16*, 122–136.

Ladson-Billings, G. (2002). I ain't writin' nuttin': Permissions to fail and demands to succeed in urban classrooms. In L. Delpit & J. K. Dowdy (eds.), *The skin that we speak: Thoughts on language and culture in the classroom* (pp. 107–120). New York: The New Press.

Louis, K. S., Marks, H. M., & Kruse, S. (1996). Teachers' professional community in restructuring schools. *American Educational Research Journal, 33*, 757–798.

Mullen, C. A., & Hutinger, J. L. (2008). The principal's role in fostering collaborative learning communities through faculty study group development. *Theory Into Practice, 47*, 276–285.

Neumerski, C. M. (2013). Rethinking instructional leadership, a review: What do we know about principal, teacher, and coach instructional leadership, and where should we go from here. *Educational Administration Quarterly, 49*, 310–347.

Olivier, D. F., & Hipp, K. K. (2006). Leadership capacity and collective efficacy: Interacting to sustain student learning in a professional learning community. *Journal of School Leadership, 16*, 505–519.

Robinson, V. M. J., Lloyd, C. A., & Rowe, K. J. (2008). The impact of leadership on student outcomes: An analysis of the differential effects of leadership types. *Educational Administration Quarterly, 44*(5), 635–674.

Schein, E. H. (1992). *Organizational culture and leadership*. San Francisco, CA: Jossey-Bass.

Uline, C. L., Tschannen-Moran, M., & Wolsey, T. D. (2009). The walls still speak: The stories occupants tell. *Journal of Educational Administration, 47*, 400–426.

Uline, C. L., Wolsey, T. D., Tschannen-Moran, M., & Lin, C. (2010). Improving the physical and social environment of school: A question of equity. *Journal of School Leadership, 20*, 597–632.

Access to Challenging Curricula for All Students

Our demographics do not give us permission to offer our students less than students get in wealthier communities. In fact, our demographics demand that we teach more so that we give our students realistic opportunities to compete in life. Our students will learn more only if we structure our classes so that students learn content that is just as rigorous as the content learned in schools in wealthy communities. Why not give our students the same challenges, the same opportunities? If we don't, who will?

Magdalena Aguilar, Former Principal, Escontrias Elementary,
Socorro Independent School District, El Paso, TX

While evidence of a positive transformational culture was abundant throughout the high-performing urban schools, the site visit teams also found substantial evidence of rich, balanced curricula that challenged students to develop deep understandings of important concepts. Educators in the high-performing urban schools worked to ensure that all students, and all demographic groups of students, had strong opportunities to master key concepts. Access to challenging curricula profoundly influenced the achievement of excellent and equitable learning results. Students from all demographic groups learned more rigorous academic content, in large part, because they were taught more rigorous content.

Focus on Deep Understanding

Even before states and districts adopted more challenging academic standards (e.g., Common Core State Standards, Next Generation Science Standards), the award-winning schools focused on getting students to demonstrate a depth of understanding related to key academic topics. Students were expected to analyze relationships, distinguish differences, apply concepts to solve real problems, and utilize rubrics to evaluate their own learning. This is not intended to suggest that these high-performing schools avoided memorization and lower-level cognitive tasks. We saw a range of learning objectives; however, the primary goal of instruction was ensuring students grasped, and could demonstrate, deep understanding of the curricular content and how it might be applied in various contexts.

To focus on deeper levels of understanding, often teachers pushed beyond the knowledge required by problems in the textbook or in district curricular materials.

Sometimes, teachers pushed beyond the depth of knowledge required by state standards. For example, instead of asking students simply to find an answer in the text, teachers expected students to explain why an answer made sense. Teachers expected students to do more than "solve for x." They wanted students to be able to explain why the solution was logical and how the solution could be applied to real-life situations.

Teachers wanted students to learn more than dates and timelines. They also wanted students to be able to explain the relationships between the dates and the various events that populated the timeline.

To address more rigorous academic standards, teachers in many high-performing urban schools paid close attention to the verb that defined what students were expected to master. For example, when the standard specified that students should be able to estimate, teachers planned lessons that required students to demonstrate their ability to estimate well. Similarly, when the standard specified that students should be able to construct something (e.g., a set of charts that explain a phenomenon), teachers planned instruction to ensure that students possessed the necessary content knowledge to construct the product well. Also, they worked to make sure that students had sufficient experiences constructing the product. Additionally, they often provided students opportunities to evaluate their product or products developed by others, using explicit criteria associated with the standard.

Teachers in the high-performing schools did not reduce the level of rigor implied by the standard. For instance, they did not allow students simply to recall information if the standard indicated that students should be able to make appropriate inferences. Teachers would not conclude instruction when students could add fractions if the standard required that students be able to model the addition of fractions. Rather, teachers would persist to ensure that students could model the operation appropriately. In many cases, discussions in collaborative planning meetings helped teachers focus on the level of rigor implied by the verb associated with the standard. This focus on the rigor of standards was made easier, because educators were attending to fewer standards than they had addressed in prior years.

Through the adoption of Common Core or similar sets of standards, many states have greatly reduced the number of standards teachers are expected to teach. Even before states adopted these new sets of standards, we witnessed teachers in high-performing schools determining that they would focus upon a smaller set of the most important standards in each discipline. They deliberately did not try to "cover" every topic or teach every objective. By focusing upon a smaller set of critical standards, teachers were able to dedicate the time necessary to ensure that all children, and all groups of children, developed deep understandings of important, challenging academic content.

Writing to Promote Understanding

In high-performing urban schools, teachers spent considerable time engaging students in writing explanations, narratives, arguments, opinions, and other text types that helped teachers gauge how well students understood a concept. Yes, teachers spent considerable time teaching writing in English or literacy classes. However, they also required students to write in almost every other subject area.

For example, middle school students at Horace Mann Dual Language Magnet School in Wichita, Kansas wrote speeches for Abraham Lincoln for the purpose of convincing citizens to reject efforts to cede from the union. Elementary students at Dr. Charles Lunsford School in Rochester, New York composed friendly letters to peers, explaining how to solve real-life problems using multiple-step arithmetic. Students at Lawndale High School in the Los Angeles area created a version of Shakespeare's *King Lear* that their peers would easily understand and appreciate. In each case (and many others), teachers engaged students in writing assignments aimed at demonstrating their deeper understanding of the academic content across the curriculum.

In many high-performing urban schools, students completed writing assignments frequently. Often, examples of student writing filled bulletin boards and lined hallways. Teachers used writing as a vehicle for helping ensure that students understood challenging concepts across a wide array of subject areas.

Access to Art, Music, Physical Education, and Other Non-Tested Subjects

Students with greater academic needs were not relegated to a daily schedule that included a triple dose of math and a quadruple dose of reading, while more successful students experienced art, instrumental music, drama, engineering, science, robotics, dance, chorus, etc. Leaders made sure that all students experienced the joy of a rich, broad curriculum.

Contrary to popular myths, students in high-performing urban schools had access to rich curricula that included science, the arts, technology, physical education, world languages, and other topics beyond the focus of most state testing programs. High achievement on standardized tests was not a result of narrow attention to mathematics and reading. Elementary, middle, and high schools offered exciting programs that allowed students to explore and develop their interests and abilities. Many of the high-performing urban schools featured programs that helped students develop second languages, perform Shakespearean plays, learn computer coding, develop television productions, and engage in other learning tasks that made school exciting, interesting, and fun.

Often English, mathematics, science, and social science teachers thoughtfully integrated co-curricular or extra-curricular content with core academic instruction. Similarly, teachers in extra-curricular areas often integrated important math, science, and literacy skills into their lessons and activities. For example, we found art teachers giving students practical opportunities to utilize concepts of congruence and symmetry that they were learning in geometry lessons. We saw history teachers engaging students in dramatizations of historic debates. Math teachers helped students understand fractions by listening to music and reading notes in a musical measure. Physical education teachers reinforced multiplication facts by altering the number of points associated with a goal or a score.

It is important to note that high-performing schools provided valuable opportunities for all students, and all groups of students, to experience rich and balanced curricula. Students with greater academic needs were not relegated to a daily schedule that included a triple dose of math and a quadruple dose of reading, while more successful students experienced art, instrumental music, drama, engineering, science, robotics, dance, chorus, etc. Leaders made sure that all students experienced the joy of a rich, broad curriculum.

Rigor for All Students

It is important to note that educators in the high-performing schools provided all students access to challenging curricula, not just those deemed academically talented or gifted. Students who struggled with a particular objective because of a lack of grade-level reading ability, challenges at home, or a disability were generally expected to master the same curricular goals as did other students. For English learners, whether instruction was provided in the students' native language or in English, the learning goal was generally the same as the goal for students whose first language was English. Teachers might have used different strategies, more examples, more personalized assistance, additional uses of technology, etc., but the typical aim was to get all students to master the same challenging academic goals.

Often teachers taught students in heterogeneous groups, ensuring that all students had the opportunity to learn key academic content. Oakes' (1985) seminal study on student tracking discredited a common belief that students learn better among similar-ability peers, and that teachers are more successful teaching similar-ability students. Her research further revealed disturbing trends regarding ability groupings and race, with Latino and African American students more often assigned to lower tracks, resulting in diminished access to high-quality learning experiences. In high-performing schools, instruction was planned in a manner that was sensitive to the diverse strengths and needs of students contained within purposefully heterogeneous groups. Lessons were designed to maximize the likelihood that every student, and all groups of students, would master the content. Also, teachers sought and utilized feedback from students to modify and adapt lessons (sometimes in midstream) so that more students would succeed. At times, teachers would use student feedback to determine which students needed extra help and which students needed extended learning opportunities.

On occasions when teachers taught in homogeneous groups, groupings were based on the specific concept or skill the students needed to master (not based on general notions of "ability"). By identifying a group that needed to master a specific concept or skill, the teacher could address the issue quickly and accelerate students' re-integration with the class.

The Power of a Coherent Educational Improvement System to Ensure Curricular Rigor for All Students

Widespread access to curricular rigor resulted from carefully constructed structures, routines, policies, and norms. Access was carefully scheduled, planned, monitored, and adjusted. In the absence of this careful, systemic attention, it is likely that many students would not have enjoyed the opportunity to learn challenging academic content.

Leading Stakeholders to Feel Valued and Capable

Teachers in high-performing schools experienced sufficient systemic support from their leaders and colleagues so that they were willing to try to teach more challenging academic concepts. In many schools, teachers expressed their belief that they could risk teaching new, difficult concepts because failure was not punished. In fact, efforts to teach challenging concepts were respected and appreciated. As a teacher at Jim Thorpe Fundamental School in Santa Ana, California explained:

> At my last school, I would have never tried to get my students to explain their thinking in writing, the way I do here. First, my principal would have said that I was wasting my time and the other teachers would have accused me of trying to show off. If I succeeded nobody would have appreciated it, and if I failed I would have been humiliated. Probably, I would have been humiliated, either way. Here [at Jim Thorpe], if I try, my principal will observe me and leave me a note to congratulate me for trying, whether I succeed or not.

Support from colleagues in PLCs or other collaborative teams, support from leaders through observations and feedback, and support from a variety of sources through professional development were powerful in helping educators feel that they could safely try to teach more challenging academic skills to the diverse populations they served. Teachers were more willing to try to teach difficult concepts and, as a result, students were more likely to learn.

Leading Educators to Develop a Focus on Teaching a Set of Important, Challenging Concepts and Skills

To ensure that all students (and all demographic groups of students) accessed challenging academic curricula, educators worked together to identify the rigorous standards they would teach and schedule when those standards would be taught. As a team, teachers (often working with administrators) identified the standards that would be the focus of instruction, developed a shared understanding of the learning outcomes students should be able to demonstrate, and set a timeline that specified when students would demonstrate mastery of the concepts and skills. Sometimes this work occurred during teacher collaboration meetings or grade-level team meetings. At other times, the planning involved vertical teams of teachers who taught the same discipline.

Often, during planning meetings, teachers discussed the standards and the specific knowledge and skills specified or implied. Through these detailed conversations, teachers developed a common understanding of the content students would need to access. For example, in one planning meeting, an elementary teacher explained:

> No, it is not enough for the students to label the numerator and the denominator. They need to understand that if the numerator stays the same and the denominator gets bigger, the fraction gets smaller. That's a hard concept for third graders.

By developing a common understanding of the rigorous content students need to learn, teachers helped ensure that they would each give students similar access to challenging concepts. In the absence of these detailed discussions about the standards, it might have been easy for teachers to proceed with varying ideas about what their students needed to learn.

At Boone Elementary in Kansas City, Missouri's Central School District, teachers took Common Core State Standards and developed clear "I can" statements that articulate what students are expected to learn. In order to generate these clear, short statements, teachers had to reach consensus about what the standards meant. Also, by translating the standards into "I can" statements, teachers were able to communicate the standards effectively to parents and students.

In many schools, vertical-planning structures enhanced access to curricular rigor for all students, connecting learning expectations horizontally within and across content areas and contexts, as means to develop accurate frameworks of knowledge (Dumont, Istance, & Benavides, 2010). At regular intervals, teachers met with their colleagues from different grade levels to examine each other's plans for teaching academic standards. In elementary schools, teachers met with their colleagues in adjacent grades to discuss their plans for teaching standards associated with specific academic disciplines. For example, at Myrtle S. Finney Elementary in Chula Vista, California, teachers begin teaching close reading strategies to kindergarten students. At each subsequent grade level, teachers build upon this strategy in ways that have resulted in high rates of reading proficiency.

In secondary schools, teachers met in departments to discuss the standards they planned to teach across a sequence of courses. For instance, at James Pace Early College High School in Brownsville, Texas, math teachers worked together to help make sure that ninth-grade math offerings would lead high percentages of students to be prepared for high-level math offerings (including college algebra) by the time students entered twelfth grade.

Also, vertical planning helped teachers identify and question both duplications and gaps in their vertical articulation of learning expectations. For example, planning meetings might lead a group of elementary math teachers to discover that third-grade teachers were addressing several math topics with the same level of rigor expected by second-grade teachers. The discovery might move teachers to explore options for elevating expectations for the third-grade students.

Conversely, a planning meeting might lead high school social studies teachers to realize that their writing expectations for juniors and seniors were dramatically beyond the writing expectations for freshmen and sophomores. In response, teachers might elevate the rigor of writing expectations for sophomores so that students might have a higher likelihood of experiencing success when they reached eleventh grade.

Vertical planning helped ensure that learning expectations were clear, public, and consistent throughout the school. Because of vertical planning sessions, teachers better understood what they needed to help students master in order to succeed in subsequent grades. It is important to note that in many of the high-performing schools these vertical planning systems extended beyond the school. For example, upper elementary teachers collaboratively planned with the middle school teachers who were likely to serve their students, and middle school teachers engaged in planning experiences with high school educators. Similarly, we saw powerful examples of high school teachers reaching out to college professors to learn more about the learning expectations for college freshmen in various disciplines.

By systematically bringing teachers together to identify which standards would be taught, leaders in high-performing schools also helped ensure what Marzano (2003) referred to as a viable curriculum. Marzano explained that when teachers were expected to cover too many concepts or skills, teachers would not have adequate time to teach those concepts and skills well. In such a case, even though teachers might pursue the same guaranteed curriculum, the curriculum might not be practicable or worthwhile. In the high-performing urban schools, when teachers came together to identify key standards, they also made decisions about which standards they would omit, de-emphasize, or defer to later years. Therefore, through their collaborative planning, teachers were able to create a more viable curriculum.

As teams of educators developed clarity about what their students should learn, they also developed schedules to ensure that students had opportunities to experience and learn the breadth and depth of their schools' curricula. In secondary schools, leaders used master schedules as a critical tool for ensuring access to curricular rigor. Often in high-performing schools, master schedules provided more opportunities for students to benefit from a rich variety of curricular offerings. Schedules were structured so that all students had opportunities to participate in programs such as drama, art, music, physical education, world languages, computer coding, and other highly engaging areas of study. This meant that schedules had to offer sufficient time slots to address core course needs, while also providing time for electives.

Also, in elementary schools, schedules were established to ensure that all students (not just academically talented students) had frequent access to exciting learning experiences with the arts, physical education, science, and technology. Schedules allowed students to access academic support and intervention, while maintaining regular opportunities to participate in a broad array of enriching learning experiences. Additionally, in many districts (e.g., the Chula Vista Elementary School District), schedules provided sufficient, regular opportunities for teachers to meet for collaborative planning and review of student performance data. This contrasts with some schools in which students with multiple academic needs get pulled out of enriching learning experiences in order to receive academic support in reading and mathematics.

Leading Educators to Develop Clarity about How They Will Assess Student Mastery of Key Concepts and Skills

Teachers further enhanced their common understandings about what needed to be taught when they developed common formative assessments, aligned with the standards they endeavored to teach. Often these small assessments gave teachers a quick way of knowing the extent to which students achieved mastery of the standard or standards they attempted to teach. These discussions helped teachers plan for instruction with a specific end in mind. Teachers could backwards map (Wiggins & McTighe, 2005) from a common understanding of the learning goal and plan lessons that would have a high likelihood of helping students develop the depth of understanding required by the formative assessment.

By co-creating these assessments, teachers acquired an even stronger common understanding of what they needed their students to learn. The common understanding of key standards helped ensure that teachers would aim to teach the same content and objectives. Thus, as Marzano (2003) explained, teachers were more likely to provide a guaranteed curriculum, a curriculum that would guarantee all students an opportunity to learn key content, regardless of which teacher provided instruction.

Leading Educators to Improve the Effectiveness of Initial Instruction

To increase the chances that all students were able to access rigorous academic curricula, leaders in many high-performing urban schools helped teachers plan schedules that structured additional student supports into regular classrooms. For example, in these schools, students with disabilities often received support from specialists during regular class sessions. Specialists were less likely to pull students out of class and provide different curricula (pull-out model). Instead, the specialists were more likely to enter general classrooms and help students succeed with the same rigorous standards other students were learning (push-in model). Special educators used their training and skills to help students with disabilities (and other students who needed assistance) in a way that helped students learn challenging concepts. The special educators provided individualized or small-group assistance that maximized student engagement, clarified complex tasks, and provided essential accommodations. As a result, students with disabilities were more likely to demonstrate mastery of rigorous academic skills, because they were provided initial instruction with sufficient, high-quality support.

In many schools, similar in-class supports were provided to English learners. Using a push-in model, specialists helped individual students or small groups of students engage in conversations about important ideas and understand key concepts. The specialists helped ensure that English learners would not miss opportunities to learn challenging academic standards. The specialists helped ensure that access to challenging academic content would not be blocked by language differences. Initial instruction was more likely to lead English learners to mastery of challenging concepts because students had access to sufficient, high-quality support.

Leading Educators to Improve the Effectiveness of Intervention and Enrichment

As previously discussed, in high-performing urban schools, systems helped ensure that all students had access to challenging academic curricula, primarily through their general education classes. Scheduling, teacher planning, and in-classroom supports helped ensure that students had strong opportunities to learn rigorous, meaningful content. Additionally, in high-performing schools, educators developed systems for providing timely, effective intervention, as a way of further guaranteeing access to curricular rigor for all students.

When students did not demonstrate mastery of challenging academic content after initial instructional efforts, educators provided focused, timely, and effective intervention (additional access) that helped ensure that all demographic groups of students would excel. It is important to distinguish that, in these schools, intervention provided additional access to challenging curricula. This is not the case in some schools where intervention is focused almost exclusively on lower-level learning goals. In the high-performing schools, teachers (often working in collaborative teams) utilized student work products or assessment results to identify the specific misconceptions that might have inhibited student mastery of their challenging objectives. They then designed intervention that would effectively address those misconceptions in a timely, efficient manner.

Intervention was not a separate support or separate system; it was part of *the* system for ensuring that all students mastered the academic goals teachers had targeted for them. Often, the teacher who provided intervention was the same teacher who provided the initial instruction. When a different teacher provided intervention, the system provided for strong communication between the teachers, so that intervention would be tailored in a way that was likely to be effective. Groupings for intervention tended to be fluid because a student who needed help mastering one concept might not need assistance mastering the next concept. As well, the physical structure of interventions (time of day, location) was designed carefully to ensure that the students who needed assistance would have a high likelihood of receiving it, without risking their access to other important curricular content.

Summary

Teachers in high-performing urban schools worked together to ensure that all students had opportunities to learn challenging academic content determined to be critical for students at the particular grade level, or in the particular subject area. The high-performing urban schools we studied could not have achieved the results they attained without providing this access. Specifically, educators in these high-performing urban schools engaged in the following practices:

♦ Teachers worked together to identify the most important concepts and skills within the discipline they were teaching. They aligned their choices to state standards; however, they sometimes went beyond state standards if they perceived that their students needed to learn more rigorous content.

♦ Teachers worked to develop shared understandings of what mastery of each standard or learning objective implied for students. Teachers developed shared expectations about what students should demonstrate in order to convince teachers that mastery had been achieved.

♦ Teachers did not necessarily include every state standard or objective in what they agreed to teach (especially in years prior to the adoption of new sets of standards, such as Common Core State Standards or Next Generation Science Standards). They planned so that they could have enough time during the school year to get all of their students to master the standards they had determined were most important.

♦ In selecting standards and learning objectives, teachers aimed high. They wanted to ensure that their students learned concepts with sufficient depth of understanding to enable students to continue learning and growing in the field of study.

- ◆ Across curricula, teachers engaged students in writing. Writing provided opportunities for students to formulate and demonstrate deeper understandings of the academic content that was the focus of instruction.

- ◆ Educators made sure that all students, and all demographic groups of students, had access to rich opportunities to learn about the arts, drama, dance, technology, and other disciplines beyond the traditional core subjects.

- ◆ Educators scheduled access to ensure that all students would learn key concepts. Teachers created a "guaranteed and viable" curriculum by determining a reasonable calendar for teaching and assessing key concepts.

- ◆ Schools utilized vertical planning to help ensure that teachers taught the concepts that students needed to master in order to achieve success at the next grade level.

- ◆ By providing in-class supports (versus pull-out programs), educators had more opportunity to ensure that all students would be able to learn the challenging academic content associated with the grade level and/or subject area.

- ◆ Timely, effective intervention systems provided additional assurance that all students would learn challenging academic content.

In combination, these practices helped ensure that all groups of students had the opportunity to master important, challenging academic content. Access to challenging curricula was not assumed; it was purposefully designed and carefully monitored. Educators understood that students were not likely to learn challenging content unless they deliberately taught challenging content. So, they did so in a way that reached almost every student.

What It Is & What It Isn't: Access to Challenging Curricula for All Students

What It Is: Clear Agreement about What Will Be Taught

Teachers meet to determine which standards will be taught at each grade level and in each academic area. They don't simply identify topics to be "covered." They identify the standards they think all students should master. Furthermore, they reach agreements about what they are willing to accept as evidence that each student has achieved mastery of the standard. They reach agreements about how they will assess mastery (usually through short, common formative assessments) and they agree upon the dates those assessments will be administered. Thus, they commit to ensuring that all of their students will have opportunities to learn and master important academic content.

What It Isn't: Inconsistent Understandings about What Will Be Taught

Teachers are expected to read and understand state standards and district curriculum guides. They are expected to "cover" all standards and all curricular objectives; however, there is little clarity or consistency across teachers about what students are expected to master or what students should be able to do to demon-strate mastery. As a result, what gets "taught" is often limited to what is in the text-book or what is on the worksheet.

* * *

What It Is: Focus on Higher-Level Skills

Teachers are not content when their students merely memorize and recite. They seek evidence that every student understands the content enough to be able to explain, compare, apply, and utilize other higher-level skills. For example, a group of second-grade teachers might determine that they want their students to master subtraction well enough to be able to compute answers correctly and to be able to explain why each step of the algorithm they use makes sense.

What It Isn't: Focus on Covering Material

Teachers' primary goal is to cover the content in the district's pacing guide or scope and sequence chart. Often, depth of understanding is sacrificed so that the chapter is completed by Friday or the designated day on the curricular calendar. Most of the students who attain a real depth of understanding already knew the content before the lesson began.

* * *

What It Is: Focus on Leading Students to Master Content

Teachers design instruction to provide every student with an opportunity to achieve mastery of the same challenging academic content. Teachers ask themselves, "What will I need to do to make sure that Leticia, Jerome, and Manuel really under-stand this?" "What materials, resources, experiences, and learning activities will stu-dents need in order to master this content or skill?" When teachers utilize groupings, they do so to help ensure that every group progresses toward, and achieves mastery of, the content. Therefore, groupings are usually fluid, changing many times within a school year.

What It Isn't: Focus on Ability Grouping

Students are placed in groups that rarely change. An example occurs when stu-dents are assigned to groups by ability level for an entire semester or year. Teachers explain that they "give students the opportunity to succeed at their level"; however, academic gaps widen because students in the lower groups are assigned easier (usu-ally less interesting) tasks geared to lower-level thinking skills, the pace of instruc-tion is slower, and there is no sense of urgency for helping students catch up with grade-level expectations.

* * *

What It Is: Rich Curricula Including Art, Music, and Physical Education

The curriculum includes art, music, physical education, drama, and other areas of study that may not be tested by the state, but may provide rich opportunities to bring life to core academic subjects and make school more interesting (and yes, even fun). For example, music teachers collaborate with math teachers so that lessons related to equivalent fractions are reinforced as students learn about quarter notes, eighth notes, etc. Art lessons provide practical opportunities for students to explore the meaning of concepts such as symmetry and congruence. Robotics labs offer students opportunities to practice expository writing as they create instruction booklets to guide others in operating their mechanical creations.

What It Isn't: Curricula Limited to Core Subjects

Students get double and triple doses of core academic content so there is not room for much else. Students either learn to love challenging subjects or they learn to hate school. An example occurs when students who read below grade level are not allowed to participate in band, art, or drama because they must have one period of reading, one period of reading lab, and one period of reading in content areas.

School Self-Assessment Tool: Does Your School Provide Access to Challenging Curricula for All Students?

This self-assessment will help you determine the extent to which your school provides access to challenging curricula for all students. Consider working with a team of teachers, administrators, parents, and students to respond to these questions. (One could invite participants to provide individual ratings.) Completion of the self-assessment will generate a picture of the school's current practices. By utilizing the same process annually or semi-annually, the school can assess progress toward developing excellent access to challenging curricula for all students. Rate the following on a scale of 1 to 5, with 1 representing NOT LIKELY and 5 representing VERY LIKELY.

I. How likely is it that all teachers who teach the same grade level and/or same subject at your school will share a common commitment to teaching the same specific standards and curricular objectives throughout the school year? Rating _____

II. How likely is it that all teachers who teach the same grade level and/or same subject at your school will share a common understanding of the meaning behind each key standard they teach? Rating _____

III. How likely is it that all teachers who teach the same grade level and/or same subject at your school will use the same assessment tool to determine whether or not students have mastered key academic standards? Rating _____

IV. How likely is it that classroom observations would confirm that when teachers endeavor to teach the same content standard, they do so with a focus on the same high level of rigor? Rating _____

V. How likely is it that teachers in extra-curricular or co-curricular areas (e.g., art, music, drama) regularly integrate academic standards from core academic subjects into their lessons and activities? Rating _____

VI. How likely is it that teachers in core academic subjects regularly integrate art, music, drama, and other extra-curricular/co-curricular activities into their lessons? Rating _____

VII. To what extent does the master schedule help ensure that all students have abundant opportunities to access instruction in extra-curricular/co-curricular areas? Rating _____

VIII. How likely is it that students who need high levels of additional academic assistance will regularly participate in lessons and activities that focus on art, music, drama, and other extra-curricular/co-curricular subjects? Rating _____

IX. How likely is it that English learners will receive academic instruction, focused on the same challenging objectives taught to students who are proficient in English? Rating _____

X. How likely is it that students with mild-to-moderate disabilities will receive academic instruction, focused on the same challenging objectives taught to students who do not have disabilities? Rating

XI. When students are grouped by ability for instructional purposes, how likely is it that students will move into different groups several times during the year, as they master specific standards and objectives? Rating _____

XII. How likely is it that teachers who teach the same grade level or the same subject area agree upon which standards and objectives they will give high priority and which standards and objectives will not receive high priority? Rating _____

XIII. How likely is it that teachers in all subject areas use writing assignments to help students formulate and demonstrate deep understandings of academic content? Rating _____

XIV. To what extent do teachers meet (at least once per semester) with teachers who teach students in adjacent grade levels or subject levels to calibrate expectations and ensure that students are being prepared to access high levels of rigor throughout their schooling experience? Rating _____

XV. How likely is it that students with mild-to-moderate disabilities will receive effective learning support in their regular classroom, focused on the same rigorous academic standards being taught to students without disabilities? Rating _____

XVI. How likely is it that English learners will receive effective learning support in their regular classroom, focused on the same rigorous academic standards being taught to students who are proficient in English? Rating _____

XVII. When students need assistance that requires them to be pulled out of the regular classroom, how likely is it that the assistance will not reduce their access to the academic content taught in the regular classroom? Rating _____

XVIII. How likely is it that teachers will identify which students need intervention or additional assistance within five days after the conclusion of instruction on a specific objective? Rating _____

XIX. When teachers identify students for intervention, how likely is it that the intervention will focus on the student's specific misconceptions or errors? Rating _____

XX. When teachers identify students for intervention, how likely is it that, after intervention, students will demonstrate mastery of the specific standards/objectives that were the focus of instruction? Rating _____

References

Dumont, H., Istance, D., & Benavides, F. (2010). *The nature of learning: Using research to inspire practice*. Paris, France: OECD.

Marzano, R. J. (2003). *What works in schools: Translating research into action*. Alexandria, VA: Association for Supervision and Curriculum Development.

Oakes, J. (1985). *Keeping track: How schools structure inequalities*. New Haven, CT: Yale University Press.

Wiggins, G., & McTighe, J. (2005). *Understanding by design*, 2nd ed. Alexandria, VA: Association for Supervision and Curriculum Development.

Effective Instruction that Results in Engagement and Mastery

4

If I just have them [my students] do what's in the textbook, they probably won't understand. I've got to figure out how to make it come to life for them. Somehow, I've got to make it real to them.

Teacher, Franklin Towne Charter High, Philadelphia, PA

In our school, we just don't give up . . . as long as a problem continues, we will continue to address it.

Teacher, Marble Hill High School, Bronx, NY

They [the teachers] don't give up on us. They think we're smart. That makes you want to work hard. I don't want to let my teachers down.

Student, William Dandy Middle School, Fort Lauderdale, FL

My daughter would do anything for that teacher. She [the teacher] has built a bond with my child in just a few months. But, that's like all the teachers here. They just care.

Parent, Golden Empire Elementary, Sacramento, CA

Across the many high-performing urban schools awarded and studied, we observed many different instructional strategies. While varied, these instructional approaches shared a common positive impact on student learning. Classroom instruction was designed and implemented in a way that resulted in students achieving high rates of mastery. High percentages of students, and high percentages of the various demographic groups served, demonstrated mastery of the challenging academic content taught. To achieve excellent and equitable learning results, not only did teachers provide a guaranteed and viable curriculum that offered students access to challenging academic content, they also provided effective instruction that resulted in high rates of engagement and mastery.

Effective instruction, in this context, does not refer to a style of teaching, a fad, trend, or method. Instead, effective instruction means instruction that resulted in the students demonstrating that they grew closer to mastering the content the teacher endeavored to teach. While we noted common practices across many high-performing schools, we also noted that effective instruction was highly contextualized because teachers tailored instruction to increase the levels of mastery of all students and all student groups.

In order to be effective, instruction had to engage all the students served. To be effective with English learners; students who had histories of behavior challenges; high achievers and low achievers; Black, Asian, Latino, White, and Native American students; recent immigrants; foster children; students with perfect attendance and students with frequent absences; students living in homeless situations and students living in affluence; students with mild, moderate, and even severe disabilities; students with gang affiliations, students considered gifted or talented; or any other group, instruction was not likely to be effective unless it engaged students.

Brown and Saks (1986) noted that instruction is more likely to lead to learning when students are provided adequate instructional time and when students attend to the instruction provided; however, engagement is more than attending behavior. When students are engaged, they are actively involved in the process of learning the targeted knowledge or skills. In high-performing schools, students are involved mentally and sometimes emotionally and physically. Engagement is not passive. Throughout our visits to high-performing urban schools, we observed students doing far more than looking at the teacher or staring in the direction of the white board. We saw students observing, measuring, writing descriptions, designing, performing, and teaching each other.

As they endeavored to create effective lessons, we saw teachers establishing stimulating learning environments that engaged students through discussions, debates, expeditions, experiments, movement, music, mobile technology, and dramatizations. We saw teachers involving students in local events, cultural activities, and other real-world experiences students perceived as interesting and relevant. We saw minimal reliance on textbooks and even fewer uses of worksheets. Instead, teachers designed excursions, projects, data hunts, and other engaging learning opportunities that were likely to result in students' mastery of the desired content. Observers noted that they heard students' voices more often than they heard teachers' voices. Teachers were constantly checking to determine what students understood or misunderstood. Teachers were constantly challenging themselves to design lessons that students were likely to perceive as interesting, engaging, and exciting.

Providing effective, engaging instruction for diverse populations of students is not the tradition of public schools and is especially not the tradition of urban public schools. In contrast, traditional instruction in the United States could be characterized as teachers presenting information and students listening quietly. Many school leaders tend to perceive adults who present academic content accurately as effective teachers; however, if we measure effectiveness by the extent to which students engage in and master the content taught, some accurate presenters of academic content may not be very effective.

Traditionally, when teachers have provided accurate presentations of information and their students have not demonstrated mastery, we have blamed the students for not listening, not studying, or not caring. We have blamed parents for not reinforcing the importance of learning, or for not helping their child (or making their child) learn. We have blamed poverty, society, and government. We have blamed teachers who taught earlier grades or different academic subjects. These heaps of blame have failed to generate improved learning results for diverse populations of students. In contrast, in the high-performing urban schools studied, we saw educators who faced all of the challenges associated with educating low-income, diverse populations of students. Instead of responding with blame, they faced these challenges with a set of instructional practices designed to engage students and lead them to master challenging academic content.

Common Practices

We found that effective instruction, while varied and driven by context, included some specific common practices. We described these common practices in our book *Teaching Practices from America's Best Urban Schools*. As illustrated in Figure 4.1, the book emphasized the eight teaching practices that were commonplace across high-achieving urban schools. While each of these teaching practices contributed to engaging, effective instruction, we noted that the focus on mastery was central to teaching efforts. Similarly, we found that all of the practices were grounded in efforts to lead all students to feel valued and capable.

Figure 4.1. **Teaching Practices in America's Best Urban Schools**

Introducing Content Logically, Clearly, and Concisely

Connecting with Students' Interests, Backgrounds, and Cultures

Focusing on Mastery

Acquiring and Responding to Evidence of Understanding

Making Students Feel Valued and Capable

Leading Students to Love Learning

Building Student Vocabulary

Promoting Successful Practice

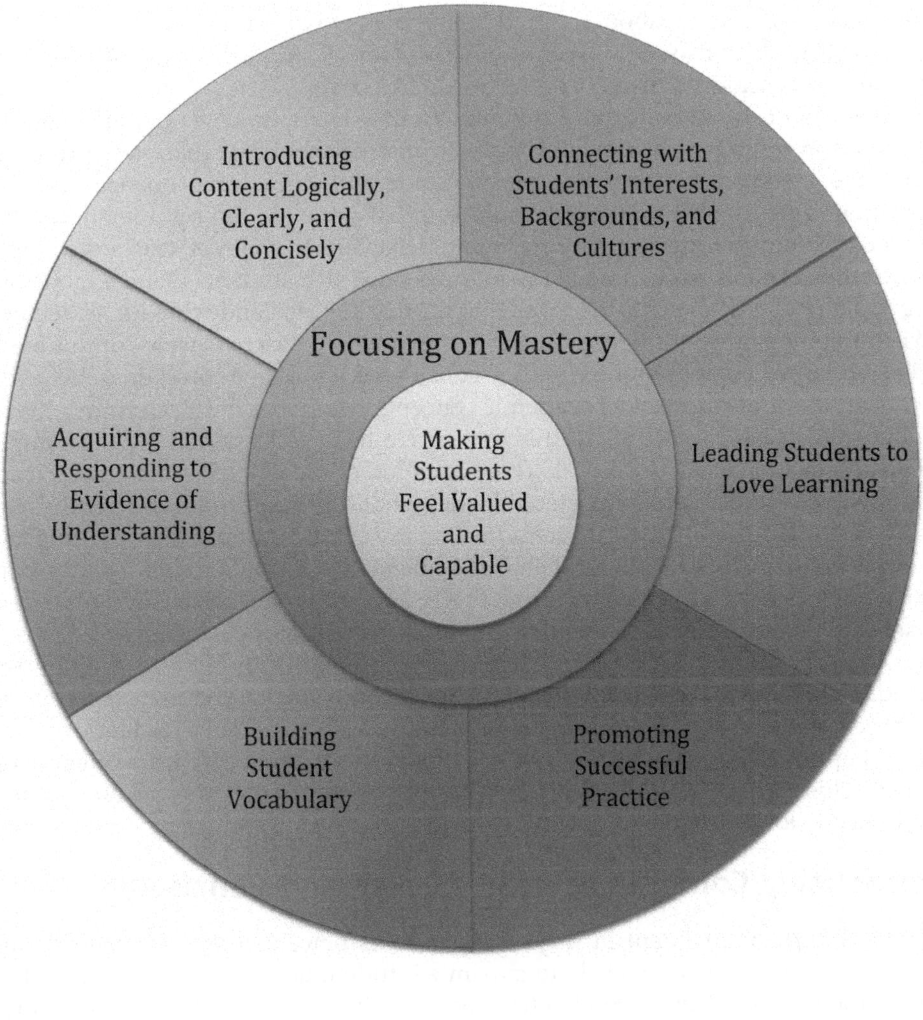

The eight teaching practices can be summarized as follows.

Focusing on Mastery

Teachers did not rely upon teacher guides, textbooks, or old lesson plans to direct the course of their lessons. Instead, lessons were driven by the teacher's commitment to ensuring that their students achieved mastery of the lesson objective.

Teachers in high-performing schools were passionate about ensuring that students acquired deep levels of mastery of the concepts and skills taught. Teachers meticulously planned lessons to lead each and every student to mastery of the lesson objectives. Teachers posted lesson objectives, not simply to comply with a principal's directive, but to articulate ambitious commitments about what their students would learn. Teachers worked relentlessly, not simply to present lessons, but to ensure that all students mastered the essential concepts and skills associated with the lessons. Throughout lessons, teachers carefully monitored what students understood related to the lesson objective and sometimes adjusted lesson designs midstream in order to increase the likelihood that every student achieved mastery. Teachers did not rely upon teacher guides, textbooks, or old lesson plans to direct the course of their lessons. Instead, lessons were driven by the teacher's commitment to ensuring that their students achieved mastery of the lesson objective.

A focus on mastery is quite different from a focus on coverage that may be observed in more typical urban schools. In many schools, teachers feel driven to cover the lesson associated with a pacing guide or a scope and sequence chart. "If someone came in my room, they would see that I was on the right lesson on the right day," some teachers might proclaim defensively. In contrast, teachers in high-performing schools were more likely to focus on which students were demonstrating mastery of the concepts they were attempting to teach and what issues seemed to be inhibiting other students from achieving mastery. Teachers were continuously engaged in processes of inquiry as they considered what they could do to help students demonstrate mastery of academic concepts. They sought to determine: "Who understands each component of this lesson? Do they understand how the components interact to create an accurate representation of the whole? Is this lesson leading my overage students to mastery? If not, what do I need to do differently? Are my most academically gifted students finding my extra-credit activities exciting and worth pursuing? If not, how can I challenge them? How can I be sure that my English learners are deriving meaning from this lesson? How can I use their heritage languages in ways that increase the likelihood that they master the lesson objectives?"

A spirit of inquiry was critical, because helping students achieve deep understandings of content was often not easy. As teachers pushed themselves to ensure that their students developed deep understandings of challenging academic content (see Chapter 3), they recognized that traditional lesson strategies were often insufficient. This spirit of inquiry often led teachers to embrace the other seven practices described below.

Introducing Content Logically, Clearly, and Concisely

By introducing content in ways that students perceived as clear, logical, and concise, lessons were more likely to maximize student understanding. As a student at Dayton Business Technology High School explained, "The teachers break it down so it makes sense and you can understand. I don't know why my teachers at the other school didn't do that."

Working in teams, teachers deconstructed complicated concepts, algorithms, and processes. They worked together to consider how they could make the complex seem logical and understandable. They planned the introduction of concepts in ways that might help students avoid common misunderstandings. As they planned, they recognized that textbooks often omitted important steps or quickly glossed over critical ideas. In some cases, they found that students were being asked to climb a ladder of understanding on which multiple rungs were missing. In more traditional classrooms, students would likely fail or pass through with partial understanding. In these high-performing schools, students thrived because teachers constructed lessons with rungs added exactly where students needed them most.

Teachers avoided lengthy lectures, choosing instead to spend a high percentage of lesson time engaging students in meaningful interaction with the lesson content. If teachers lectured at all, lectures were quick and interesting. Lessons were designed to engage students in activity that would deepen students' understanding.

Acquiring and Responding to Evidence of Understanding

Frequently, teachers checked to ensure that students understood the content being taught. In more typical classrooms, teachers might ask a question and call upon one or two students to provide the answer. Similarly, some teachers might end a long lecture with the seldom answered "Any questions?" In contrast, in the high-performing urban schools, teachers used a variety of strategies to determine what each student understood related to the lesson content. Fisher and Frey (2007) direct teachers to utilize a myriad of questioning techniques, writing tasks, projects, performances, and tests to acquire high-quality information about what students understand, misunderstand, or are yet to understand. In the schools we studied, teachers constantly asked questions and encouraged student responses. Teachers generously peppered their lessons with questions, such that students were frequently offering explanations, describing details, making inferences, offering opinions, and building deeper understandings of the lesson content. Often, teachers called upon specific students to answer, even when students had not raised their hands. After one student answered, a teacher might turn to another student and ask him or her to share their perspective. Students perceived a greater need to pay attention because they could not predict when the teacher was going to ask them to respond.

McKenzie and Skrla (2011) explained that "teachers need to know which students are and are not engaged in thinking about the instructional objective being taught" (p. 43). They explained that teachers needed to assess the active cognitive engagement of all their students. In the high-performing urban schools we studied, we observed teachers engaging a wide range of practices to determine the level of active cognitive engagement of their students.

Frequent questions prompted high levels of student engagement and also helped teachers determine what students understood. For example, by asking various students to share their thinking behind an algebra problem that most students solved incorrectly, an Eastwood Middle School teacher (in the Ysleta Independent School District in El Paso, Texas) was able to determine that most students did not understand the question imbedded in the problem. By getting students to discuss openly what the problem meant and what they were attempting to solve, the teacher helped students see that they had structured the equation incorrectly. Frequent questioning did more than prompt engagement. It also helped teachers assess levels of understanding and adapt instruction accordingly.

Often classroom discussions provided rich opportunities for teachers to acquire a better sense of what students were thinking. For example, at Kearny School of International Business, students in an English class discussed the memoir *The Glass Castle* through a Socratic seminar. During their discussion about the book, the teacher rarely spoke. Sometimes, the teacher asked students questions, but more frequently, students called upon each other to share their opinions and insights. While students engaged in this focused, text-driven discussion, the teacher made notes about student comments. The teacher was then able to ask probing questions that led specific students to think more deeply about important story elements.

Similarly, teachers frequently used student writing as a window into students' thinking about important concepts, processes, and ideas. As students wrote short explanations, clarifications, directions, or provided other short answers, teachers circulated throughout the room and observed students, while commenting on student work and probing for deeper responses.

To acquire feedback from many students, teachers used a variety of strategies. For example, we rarely observed teachers asking one student to approach the front of the classroom to solve a problem at the board. This traditional classroom technique allows a teacher to determine one student's level of understanding while 30 others sit dormant. Instead, in high-performing urban schools, we saw classrooms in which students used individual whiteboards so that each student could simultaneously solve the problem. Then, the teacher circulated around the room to watch students solve the problem and/or the teacher asked all students to raise their whiteboards simultaneously to show their answers. Not only was every child engaged in solving the problem, but the teacher also acquired useful information about each student's ability to understand and solve the problem.

Similarly, we observed many teachers using various forms of technology to acquire information about student understanding. For example, in many classrooms, we observed students using laptop computers, iPads, iPods, and other electronic devices to acquire instantaneous feedback about student understanding. Also, in some schools, teachers used clickers and other electronic voting devices to monitor information about student understanding. By acquiring timely information about what students were thinking, teachers were able to better tailor instruction so that all students were more likely to achieve mastery.

Teachers listened attentively to student responses, carefully read student writing, and watched deliberately as students performed assigned tasks. Teachers were eager to understand if students understood key concepts, if students could articulate the relationships between ideas, and if students could provide in-depth explanations. As teachers acquired information about student understanding, they used the information to refine lessons (often immediately) in ways that increased student understanding.

Connecting with Student Interests, Backgrounds, Cultures, and Prior Knowledge

As teachers pursued challenging academic objectives, they planned and delivered lessons that resonated with their students. Students were more likely to understand and master lesson objectives because they saw connections between the lesson content and their interests, backgrounds, cultures, and prior knowledge. Students were less likely to perceive new concepts as foreign and more likely to believe that they had the capacity to master new objectives. Gay (2010) described this type of teaching as culturally responsive pedagogy. Teachers provided instruction that was responsive to, and reflective of, the cultures and backgrounds of the students served. Such culturally responsive/relevant teaching practice "hones and develops the knowledge and skills each student already possesses, while at the same time adding new knowledge and skills to that base" (Delpit, 1995, p. 67). Teachers who employ culturally responsive teaching strategies build strong connections with each of their students (Ladson-Billings, 1994). As teachers endeavor to inspire their students, listen actively to their contributions, understand their difficulties, and expect them to always do their best, these relationships flourish (Kunjufu, 2002).

It is important to note that teachers consistently maintained these high expectations, focusing on the same standards and objectives mandated by their states and school districts. However, teachers employed strategies, techniques, and resources that students recognized as familiar. For example, at James Pace Early College High School in Brownsville, Texas, teachers frequently provided a word or idiom in Spanish to help students understand a concept being discussed in English. They reminded students about cognates so they could use their knowledge of Spanish to help master challenging concepts in English. At Whitefoord Elementary in Atlanta, a teacher used the view of neighborhood streets outside her classroom's second-story window to help students understand concepts such as perpendicular and intersecting. The aforementioned class of Lawndale High English students developed a deeper understanding of *King Lear* by "translating" the play into language their friends would be more likely to understand. For example, one student told his classmates, "You can't leave the word 'sepulcher' in there. Kids aren't going to know that word. How about 'crypt'? They've seen scary movies. They'll know what that means."

Creating culturally relevant lessons was not simply about utilizing language background, ethnic traditions, or neighborhood features to help teach concepts. Teachers also made lessons culturally relevant by utilizing popular games, television shows, movies, and social media sites to help them teach rigorous academic standards. For example, another teacher at James Pace Early College High School in Brownsville used video clips from popular television shows like *Grey's Anatomy* to give students experiences distinguishing soliloquys, monologues, dialogue, and asides before they did so using Shakespeare's *Romeo and Juliet*.

Frequently, teachers in high-performing schools operated under the assumption that their students were more likely to learn if they actively engaged in projects. Thus, at Southside Elementary in Miami, teachers designed every lesson around an object that students could see, touch, hear, and experience. At World of Inquiry Elementary in Rochester, New York, lessons in various content areas were designed as part of multi-faceted projects that students found exciting. Educators created interdisciplinary learning expeditions, established partnerships with local experts, and constructed units that resulted in the development and presentation of authentic products. At Dayton Business and Technology High School, teachers collectively committed to ensuring that every lesson contained an experiential component related to real-world phenomena. Without relying upon textbooks and worksheets, teachers introduced challenging academic standards within the context of vibrant and enriching experiences that encouraged a love of, and excitement for, learning.

We know they [our students] can achieve anything. We just have to find a way to get them to learn it.

Teacher, Escontrias Elementary, El Paso, TX

Teachers assumed that their students could learn difficult academic concepts if they found ways to help their students see the connections between the concepts and their various backgrounds, experiences, cultures, and prior knowledge. We heard several teachers make statements similar to the comment articulated by a teacher at Escontrias Elementary in the Socorro Independent School District in El Paso who said, "We know they [our students] can achieve anything. We just have to find a way to get them to learn it." This belief in the capacity of students to succeed with rigorous content was key to student success. In large part, this belief fueled the teachers' search for lesson ideas that were not likely to be found in teacher guides or district curriculum materials. Teachers used their knowledge of their students, the students' families, and the students' backgrounds to create lessons that led students to think, "Oh, yes! I know about this. This makes sense to me."

Building Student Vocabulary

In high-performing urban schools, teachers generated high levels of student engagement with rigorous academic content. To this end, teachers chose to help students engage with the vocabulary that was central to the content. This does not mean teachers simply identified and taught vocabulary words. More specifically, it means that teachers helped students become comfortable using the vocabulary associated with the lesson content. It means that teachers helped students integrate the lesson vocabulary into their speaking vocabulary.

In more typical schools, vocabulary instruction rarely involves students speaking and using the vocabulary. Frequently, students are asked to write the vocabulary words, read them, find definitions, and perhaps write a sentence about the words. While we found some teachers who used these techniques, teachers were deliberate about making sure that students used the vocabulary multiple times in conversations.

This approach to helping students master key vocabulary was a prominent instructional routine in many high-performing schools. For example, at Columbus Elementary in Glendale, California, classroom aides were trained to help small groups of students practice the use of key lesson vocabulary. The aides would introduce a word in the context of a sentence or a story. They would talk about the word's meaning and then they would ask questions that prompted students to use the word. One aide introduced the word "astonished" and talked about the word's definition. Then the aide prompted the students to use the word in simple responses. "How would you feel if a kid brought an elephant to school?" she asked. After students gave short, simple responses like "I'd be astonished!" the aide asked more complex questions, such as "Why would you be astonished?" or "What else might have caused you to be astonished?" The interaction was intentionally designed to get every student in the group to develop a level of comfort with each key vocabulary word.

Similarly, at MC² STEM High School in Cleveland, Ohio, a teacher introduced the concepts of compression and tension as they related to the engineering and construction of bridges. The teacher demonstrated how compression points worked and then asked students to work in teams to build their own bridges. As the students worked, the teacher circulated and asked students questions that required them to use the terms *compression* and *tension*. If students did not respond using the key vocabulary, the teacher asked additional questions until students used the desired terms accurately.

Helping students integrate lesson vocabulary into students' spoken vocabulary was particularly important to the success of students who had never or rarely seen, heard, or spoken the vocabulary previously. To English learners, students from low-income homes, recent immigrants, students experiencing homelessness, or students whose families typically speak non-standard English dialects, the language experienced at school can be surprisingly foreign. In more typical schools, teachers act as if students will understand and utilize this vocabulary instantly. This may be as unrealistic as expecting adults to instantly understand and utilize vocabulary in an unfamiliar foreign language. In contrast, in high-performing schools, teachers provided students multiple opportunities to practice speaking new vocabulary, so that students could more easily engage in meaningful learning.

Promoting Successful Practice

Teachers allowed students to practice skills independently only when they knew that independent practice was likely to be successful. Teachers did not assign independent work if they had little reason to believe that students would be successful performing the work. Instead, lessons were carefully structured so that students experienced a balance of struggle and success that resulted in each student reaching mastery. While finding the right balance is important to the success of all students, it might be especially important for many of the diverse groups of students served in urban schools. Students who have endured a history of failure in school are much less likely to engage if they perceive that their efforts will result in one more failure experience. In high-performing urban schools, teachers generated high rates of student mastery for diverse populations of students, in part, because teachers sought and maintained the proper balance of struggle and success for each student.

Pearson and Gallagher (1983) described the importance of teachers utilizing a gradual release of responsibility. They found that students were more likely to perform academic tasks independently when teachers first modeled the performance of the task, and then performed the task jointly with students. Students were more likely to demonstrate mastery if teachers gave students responsibility for completing tasks independently only after students could perform the task with support from the teacher or from others. Saphier, Haley-Speca, and Gower (2008) explained that "guidance should be high with new tasks and withdrawn gradually with demonstrated student proficiency" (p. 231).

In more typical urban schools, one might observe teachers providing a few examples ("I'll do items 1 and 2 on the board") and then assigning students to work independently for the remainder of the class period ("Do items 3 through 30 on your own. Any questions?"). In such cases, failure rates are predictably high for students of color, English learners, students with disabilities, and other diverse groups. Under these more typical circumstances, students struggle far more than they experience success.

Alternately, in some urban classrooms, teachers reiterate far too much content from previous grade levels, failing to build students' confidence and capacity for the struggle that accompanies genuine learning. Students continue to "learn" concepts they have already learned, experiencing false success rather than mastery of new content.

In contrast, teachers in the high-performing urban schools acquired and attended to evidence of student understanding and adjusted lessons to ensure the proper gradual release of responsibility. By asking questions frequently, engaging students in discussions, asking students to perform small tasks, and correcting misconceptions early, teachers were able to monitor students' readiness to perform tasks independently. For example, when teachers at Muller Elementary in Tampa, Florida required students to respond to questions on small whiteboards, teachers could quickly monitor the student responses and determine which students were answering appropriately. By further probing and asking students to explain their answers, teachers could determine which students acquired the correct answers based on an accurate understanding of the relevant principles. With this knowledge, teachers could then determine which students had a reasonable likelihood of succeeding with a larger independent task focused upon the same academic objective.

In high-performing urban schools, teachers eliminated, or at least minimized, the time students spent performing tasks incorrectly. Students spent less time repeating errors as they wrote, calculated, read, or reasoned. Students were less likely to experience repeated academic failure and students were more likely to perceive themselves as academically capable.

Making Students Feel Valued and Capable

School personnel took great care to ensure that all students felt valued, respected, and appreciated. In every high-performing urban school studied, students reported that the adults at their school cared about them. Students shared that teachers took the time to know about them and their situations. Students indicated that administrators knew them by name. Students and parents reported that adults at the school demonstrated a level of concern and commitment that they had not experienced at other schools. Often, we heard students say, "The teachers here want us to succeed."

Of course, the overwhelming majority of educators care about their students and their students' academic success. However, in more typical urban schools, students articulate many more questions about the sincerity of the adults with whom they spend their days. In fact, in some urban schools, students are convinced that educators simply do not care about them or many of their peers. Thus, it was noteworthy that almost all students in the high-performing urban schools indicated that educators cared sincerely and deeply about their personal and academic success.

Ferguson (2002) found that students were more likely to work hard if they believed that their teacher cared about them. Additionally, Ferguson (2002) and Boykin and Noguera (2011) reported that the relationship between students' willingness to exert effort and students' perceptions of their teacher's level of care was stronger for Black and Latino students than for White students. Thus, it is not surprising that in urban schools that generated strong academic results for Black and Latino students, students reported that their teachers sincerely cared about them.

Educators demonstrated their concern and commitment in many ways. First, educators consistently interacted with students in a manner that demonstrated a high level of personal regard. Students reported that teachers interacted with them in a way that consistently demonstrated care and respect. At William Dandy Middle School in Fort Lauderdale, Florida, a student reported, "Our teachers always treat us with respect," and another student added, "Even when we don't deserve it." In the hallways, teachers greeted students by name. As students entered classrooms, teachers asked students about their families, weekend activities, college applications, sports activities, hobbies, jobs, etc. In the rare situations when behavior problems arose, teachers and other adults handled incidents calmly and respectfully.

Educators also demonstrated that they cared about and valued students by finding many ways to acknowledge and celebrate student accomplishments. Frequently, teachers made small but sincere verbal acknowledgments of positive behavior, strong effort, and significant improvement. As well, teachers celebrated excellent student work by posting it attractively and professionally in classrooms and hallways. In the high-performing urban schools, we saw recent examples of good student work products posted much more frequently than we found in typical urban schools. In high-performing elementary, middle, and even high schools, educators displayed exemplary student writing, science projects, research papers, and other work products. Principals and other school leaders conducted various activities to celebrate individual students and entire classrooms for their learning accomplishments, academic progress, behavioral successes, and extra-curricular activities. Students perceived that the adults at school were proud of them. Black students, Latino students, English learners, students with disabilities, recent immigrants, gay and lesbian students, students experiencing homelessness, foster children, and students with behavioral issues all reported that teachers and administrators wanted them to succeed.

Additionally, as described in Chapter 2, teachers in high-performing urban schools demonstrated their concern by acting as warm demanders (Bondy & Ross, 2008; Irvine & Fraser, 1998; Ladson-Billings, 2002). Educators took the time to get to know their students personally, demonstrated unconditional positive regard, and simultaneously insisted that students perform to high standards. Students reported that teachers expected them to work diligently. At the same time, students also reported that teachers provided whatever support they needed in order to successfully meet their teachers' high expectations.

Leading Students to Love Learning

Students in high-performing urban schools achieved more because teachers led them to love learning. The Professional Standards for Educational Leaders (PSEL), the new national standards for educational leaders (which replace the Interstate School Leadership Licensure Consortium Policy Standards (ISLLC)), specifically calls for school leaders to promote each student's "love of learning" (National Policy Board for Educational Administration, 2015, p. 12). In the schools we studied, students from all demographic groups mastered challenging mathematics, science, social science, English, and other subjects, in part, because teachers created lessons that the students perceived as engaging, interesting, and inspiring.

Often students became excited about learning academic content because their teachers helped them understand how the content was relevant to their current or future lives. Teachers overtly explained the importance of lesson objectives to their students or they led students to discover the importance/relevance on their own. For example, a teacher at Hambrick Middle School in Houston, Texas (Aldine Independent School District) explained to her students how they could use linear equations to make sure that their paychecks accurately accounted for their hourly wages and employee bonuses. At Horace Mann Dual Language Magnet School in Wichita, Kansas, an elementary teacher gave third-grade students a small project that helped them realize how important place value was in dividing amounts fairly between two, three, or four partners.

As teachers pursued challenging objectives, they frequently used materials that students were more likely to find interesting and relevant. For example, teachers frequently used fictional and non-fictional texts that featured characters who experienced some of the struggles they or their families had experienced. Students learned various literacy skills (finding main ideas, drawing conclusions, making inferences, etc.) while relating to characters who struggled through challenges such as poverty, discrimination, violence, transiency, or illness.

Often, students perceived lessons as relevant because teachers engaged students in interesting projects. As mentioned previously, in some schools—such as Southside Elementary in Miami, Florida; Dayton Business Technology High School in Dayton, Ohio; and World of Inquiry School in Rochester, New York—teachers committed to infusing experiential or project-based activities into every lesson. For example, students at Southside were unlikely to forget basic information about the chambers of the heart after dissecting real pig hearts in class. In many other high-performing schools, interesting projects occurred with sufficient regularity to keep students eager to come to class and seek to learn more.

Teachers also made abundant uses of technology to help inspire engagement and mastery. Teachers provided students with scores of interesting applications of technology to support their learning, including recording their oral reading on iPods, using the internet to find and critique original source documents, developing and using spreadsheets to project business earnings, utilizing microscopes to find potentially dangerous parasites in stagnant pond water near the school, and using publishing software to create posters for science fairs. By involving students in manipulating the technology to pursue solutions to meaningful problems, teachers maximized student engagement.

It is important to note, however, that some teachers generated high levels of student interest and engagement with minimal or no technology. In these classes, teachers maximized student engagement and mastery by creating frequent opportunities for students to interact with and learn from each other. Often class activities were structured so that students worked in small groups. With or without twenty-first-century technology, students were eager to work with their peers to solve problems, generate products, and learn academic content.

The Power of a Coherent Educational Improvement System to Ensure Effective Instruction

In the high-performing urban schools we studied, teachers employed effective instruction that resulted in student engagement and mastery. Many teachers regularly modeled the practices described in this chapter. In more typical urban schools, one might find several teachers who exhibit some of these practices, or one or two teachers who exhibit all of these practices. In contrast, in high-performing schools, these practices have become typical. Structures, routines, policies, and norms played substantial roles in helping leaders ensure that these practices became widespread throughout their schools.

Helping Stakeholders Feel Valued and Capable

Leaders influenced the school-wide improvement of instructional practices by providing support that teachers perceived as timely, useful, and plentiful. Frequently, teachers described the support they received from principals, instructional coaches, and other colleagues. "Yes, my principal expects a lot of us," explained a teacher at Horace Mann Dual Magnet Middle School in Wichita, Kansas, "but, he also makes sure we have whatever help we need. When you have that kind of support, you feel like you can meet high expectations." This sentiment was echoed by many teachers, who described the support they received through professional development sessions, principal observations and feedback, and through teacher collaboration meetings.

Teachers perceived that the support was timely, often because principals and other colleagues visited and observed classrooms regularly. For example, a teacher at Highland Elementary in Montgomery County, Maryland explained, "Sometimes, my principal will notice that I need something even before I notice it." She continued, "He's in my classroom so much and he's so attuned to what I am trying to accomplish. He will notice things that I need and order them before I even ask. Where else can you get that kind of support?"

By making teachers feel supported, leaders were able to maximize the extent to which teachers invested time and energy in improving instruction. "When you have leaders like this, you want to give it your all," a teacher at MacArthur Senior High in Houston's Aldine District explained. "You see how they believe in you and it makes you want to live up to their expectations."

Leading Educators to Develop a Focus on Teaching a Set of Important, Challenging Concepts and Skills

When teachers came together to specify the specific standards they would strive to have students master, often they gained clarity about what they needed to learn in order to teach their students well. By overtly specifying what students needed to be taught, teachers developed a sense of urgency about what they needed to learn in order to teach their students well. For example, a teacher at Jim Thorpe Fundamental School in Santa Ana explained,

> The more we clarified what literacy skills we wanted our students to master, the more it became clear to me that I needed to learn a lot more about teaching literacy. I went to a good college, but I didn't learn how to teach literacy today. And I wasn't by myself. My teammates were in the same boat. We started listing what we needed to learn in order to teach our students these tough standards.

In high-performing urban schools, the power of professional development is often enhanced as teachers develop clarity about what they need to learn in order to teach students challenging academic standards. By engaging teachers collaboratively in specifying which standards, learning targets, and objectives should be perceived as critical, leaders helped create a readiness for professional development.

Leading Educators to Develop Clarity about How They Will Assess Student Mastery of Key Concepts and Skills

When teachers worked together to specify how they would measure mastery of the critical learning outcomes they sought to teach, they acquired a clearer picture of what they needed to teach and they also acquired more questions about how they would teach those concepts and skills to the diverse groups of students they served. For example, one teacher at Dandy Middle School in Fort Lauderdale, Florida commented:

> When I saw the quiz my colleagues were developing to measure mastery of the genetics unit, I knew right away that I needed to up my game. I had been thinking about getting kids to be able to define terms, but they [my colleagues] wanted kids to be able to explain relationships. How was I going to teach that? So we talked right there in our team meeting about teaching strategies. We talked about what worked to get middle school kids to be able to explain relationships.

By engaging teachers in developing or adopting assessments to measure mastery, leaders increased the likelihood that teachers would recognize that traditional teaching strategies would be inadequate. Teachers felt a greater urgency to think "out of the box" about how they might help their students achieve mastery on the specific measures they were agreeing to use.

Leading Educators to Improve the Effectiveness of Initial Instruction

Collaborative planning, observation and feedback, and professional development were important tools for helping teachers improve initial instruction. While each one was significant individually, the three factors were even more powerful when integrated into a coherent educational improvement system.

1) Planning for Effective Instruction

Whether organized as grade-level teams, department teams, or work groups, these routines provided teachers regular opportunities to work together to plan lessons that were more likely to lead their students to engage in instruction and master the content. These collaborations provided opportunities for teachers to reflect deeply and critically on their own teaching practice, on the lesson content, and on the experiences and backgrounds of the learners in their classrooms. Sharing with one another in this way supported the risk taking and struggle necessary for transforming practice (Putnam & Borko, 1997).

In Chapter 3, we reported how collaboration helped teachers develop shared understandings about the specific standards they endeavored to teach. Additionally, collaboration helped teachers think through how they would teach specific standards in ways that resulted in high rates of student engagement and high levels of understanding and mastery. In the high-performing urban schools studied, teachers did not just identify worksheets, textbook pages, and supplemental resources that "covered" their instructional objectives. Instead, teachers utilized their collective knowledge of their students, their shared understanding of the standards they wished to teach, their knowledge of the content, and their knowledge of research and best practices to design lessons that had a high likelihood of leading all students to engage in the content and master concepts and skills. Planning teams endeavored to create lessons that helped students understand key concepts as a result of the initial lesson. In contrast, in struggling schools, teachers might spend less time planning initial instruction and then spend more time determining how to respond when students fail and require remediation.

In planning teams, teachers (often with the support of administrators) helped each other think about issues such as:

- ♦ What key objectives must students learn in order to master the standard?

- ♦ What will be accepted as evidence of mastery?

- ♦ How might teachers logically and concisely communicate core ideas related to the lesson objective?

- ♦ What experiences, resources, materials, etc. will students need in order to master this concept or skill?

- ♦ How might the lesson be structured so that students are less likely to develop common misconceptions?

- ♦ During the lesson, in what ways might teachers receive frequent feedback from students that might help the teacher know how to adjust the lesson?

- ♦ How might teachers engage students with lesson objectives in ways that connected with students' background, cultures, experiences, and prior knowledge?

- ♦ What questions might teachers ask students, or what small tasks might teachers ask students to complete, that signal students are ready to work independently with a reasonable likelihood of success?

- ♦ How might teachers engage students in speaking key lesson vocabulary so that students are more likely to develop fluency with important concepts?

- ♦ How might lessons be structured to maximize opportunities for students to utilize student-to-student interaction, engage with technology, or integrate learning across disciplines (including art, music, drama, and physical education)?

Teachers reported that they appreciated regular planning opportunities, because joint planning helped them prepare and implement more effective lessons. Tschannen-Moran, Uline, Hoy, and Mackley (2000) found that as teachers worked together to develop new instructional skills, they transformed individual knowledge into organizational knowledge.

Strong professional relationships between and among teachers create new norms of cooperation and begin to extend the definition of what it means to be a teacher. Teachers begin to see how their individual knowledge can be applied beyond their own classrooms to support curriculum, program, and policy. They begin to create a more expansive school culture that promotes individual growth at the same time as it advances the organization's capacity. (p. 264)

In the high-performing urban schools studied, teachers reported that their students demonstrated greater academic success with lesson objectives, because planning activities allowed them to support and be supported by their colleagues as they all worked to improve student learning across the school.

2) Observing Instruction and Providing Feedback

As mentioned in Chapter 2, in high-performing urban schools, teachers were observed and received feedback about their teaching practices more frequently than teachers in typical urban schools. Principals and other instructional leaders (including assistant principals, instructional specialists, instructional coaches, department chairs, and lead teachers) regularly observed instruction and provided feedback in ways that helped ensure that effective, engaging instruction occurred throughout the school.

Some leaders reported dedicating large portions of the school day to classroom observations. In many of the high-performing urban schools, leaders visited every classroom once a week or even more frequently. In the larger schools, principals shared observation responsibilities with assistant principals and instructional coaches. In order to create time for observing and providing feedback, some leaders intentionally left their offices at certain times of the day. They made classroom observation and feedback one of their most important job responsibilities. In some cases, district leaders helped by reducing district-level meetings and encouraging principals to spend more time in classrooms.

Importantly, observations focused on the extent to which instruction was engaging and effective for the students served. In their study of 14 principals of high-performing urban schools, Johnson, Uline, and Perez (2011) noted:

In every interview, principals spoke first, most, and most passionately about noticing the extent to which students were participating, learning, thinking, making sense, and understanding the concepts and skills being taught. Perhaps, at the most basic level, principals emphasized that they noticed whether all students were participating actively. (p. 129)

Instead of simply noticing what teachers did, leaders focused their attention on evidence of student engagement and learning. Often, during classroom observations, leaders asked students questions. For example, one principal reported, "Engagement means they are following the objective. They're on task. I ask the students three questions. 'What are you learning? Why are you learning it? How will you know you have mastered it?'"

Regular, systematic observations influenced better learning results for diverse populations of students because leaders attended specifically to whether or not English learners were making sense of the content being taught. Leaders paid attention to whether or not Black, Latino, and immigrant students were actively engaged in learning activities. Often leaders provided feedback to teachers that helped them consider how to better provide engaging, effective instruction for students with disabilities and other groups of students with special learning needs.

It is important to note that these frequent observations were not intended to serve as district or state-required evaluations. Principals rarely used long, complicated evaluation forms. Instead, they conducted short observations (often five to 15 minutes). By providing teachers with ongoing constructive feedback, principals were often able to help teachers improve their teaching performances before they conducted formal teacher evaluations.

3) Designing Professional Development

Professional development was also powerful in helping teachers provide more effective, engaging instruction. In the high-performing urban schools, professional development was designed to help teachers provide engaging, effective instruction, as described in this chapter. The professional development was systematic, because it included multiple components designed to help teachers develop proficiency with important pedagogical skills. Unlike what might be found in more typical urban schools, professional development was less likely to "cover" a wide array of topics. Professional development was less likely to provide a series of "once and done" workshops. Instead, professional development was designed to provide teachers multiple opportunities to become acquainted with an important concept, see the concept used in a classroom, ask questions, try implementing the idea, receive feedback, ask more questions, and refine implementation.

At Highland Elementary in Montgomery County, Maryland, one teacher explained, "Professional development here isn't like professional development any place else I've been. Whatever topic we address, we really focus on it until we get good at implementing it." In contrast, in more typical urban schools, teachers are less likely to have opportunities to "get good at" anything because professional development is not designed to generate successful implementation.

4) Ensuring Synergy Among Planning, Professional Development, Observation, and Feedback

In typical urban schools, collaborative planning (if it exists) is disconnected from what principals observe in classroom, and has little relationship with whatever professional development is provided. In the highest performing urban schools, we found a synergy among these elements that had a powerful influence on classroom instruction.

In high-performing schools, the issues leaders identified in their observations directly influenced the focus of professional development activities. Similarly, leaders shaped teacher collaboration discussions in ways that helped teachers plan the classroom implementation of professional development ideas. Often leaders reinforced professional development concepts by looking for implementation during classroom observations and providing constructive feedback. As well, PLCs and similar collaborative structures gave teachers additional opportunities to consider how they might refine implementation of key professional development concepts.

For example, at Jim Thorpe Fundamental Academy in Santa Ana, California, the principal's classroom observations frequently focused on issues related to quality student engagement. Teachers reported that the principal consistently provided feedback noting their successes at improving student engagement. As well, the principal often provided ideas about how they might improve the engagement of specific students or groups of students. During planning meetings, teachers were expected to help each other plan what they would do to maximize student engagement in lessons. Additionally, principal-led and teacher-led professional development sessions provided teachers specific strategies for increasing student engagement. The synergy between principal observations and feedback, the PLC, and professional development activities helped accelerate teachers' implementation of desired professional practices.

Leading Educators to Improve the Effectiveness of Intervention and Enrichment

Collaborative planning, observation and feedback, and professional development also had a powerful influence on the improvement of intervention and enrichment. Typically, in high-performing urban schools, after initial instruction, students took common assessments. The data generated from those common assessments (the student work) became the focus of teacher collaboration meetings, sometimes became the focus of additional observation and feedback, and, at times, became the focus of additional professional development.

The principal of Franklin Elementary in Bakersfield, California explained that, after assessments, she and the instructional specialist analyzed the data to determine what students learned successfully and what they still needed to learn. The principal explained that sometimes it was clear that only a small group of students did not achieve mastery. In those cases, grade-level teams would scrutinize the data to determine which students needed additional help, what did they learn well, and where were they confused. The teams would ask themselves questions about what might have confused students and they would create targeted intervention lessons for tutors (generally retired teachers) to use with specific groups of students.

Also, the Franklin principal explained that sometimes there might have been two or three teachers who succeeded in ensuring all or almost all of the students demonstrated mastery and one classroom where a large percentage of students had difficulty. In those cases, the principal asserted that there was a need for intensified observation, support, and feedback. Often, the instructional specialist would observe the teacher, offer suggestions, and provide a model lesson (focused on the same objective students did not master on the common assessment). This strategy helped build the teacher's capacity to teach the concept, but also helped ensure that the teachers' students would catch up quickly with their peers.

Finally, the Franklin principal noted that, after some assessments, it was clear that many or most students had not mastered the content. In those situations, the principal argued that it was more appropriate to address the situation as a professional development opportunity. The principal and the instructional specialist (sometimes with support from district personnel) would determine what professional development might help teachers better understand more powerful ways to engage students and lead students to master the specific concepts that had been assessed.

While the principal at Franklin clearly and succinctly articulated this triage approach to assessment results, many of the high-performing schools studied used similar approaches to help ensure that students advanced their understandings of key academic standards after initial instruction.

Summary

In high-performing urban schools, effective, engaging instruction promotes equitable and excellent learning results, because instruction is purposefully tailored to increase the likelihood that every student masters critical concepts and skills. Instruction is effective, not because it adheres to a particular philosophy or method. It is effective because it results in high rates of student engagement and student mastery.

In high-performing urban schools, teachers consistently used several practices that contributed to effective, engaging instruction. All of these practices helped ensure that all students achieved mastery of lesson content. Some of the practices (e.g., introducing content clearly, logically, and concisely; acquiring and responding to evidence of understanding; building student vocabulary; and promoting successful practice) focused on cognitive issues. Other practices (e.g., connecting with students' backgrounds, cultures, and prior knowledge; making students feel valued and capable; and leading students to love learning) addressed social-emotional concerns, while simultaneously addressing cognitive aspects of learning.

In the high-performing schools, these practices occurred regularly in most classrooms, not just a few. Coherent educational improvement systems were important in helping ensure that these practices became part of the fabric of these schools. In particular, regular classroom observations and feedback, collaborative teacher planning, and focused professional development were key elements that influenced the improvement of effective instruction throughout these schools.

What It Is & What It Isn't: Effective Instruction that Results in Engagement and Mastery

What It Is: Developing Student Clarity about Mastery

The teacher makes clear to every student what they will learn and understand. Because of the teacher's clarity, students understand what they are expected to learn as a result of the lesson, as much as they understand what they are expected to do during the lesson. The teacher engages students in discussing why it is important to master the objective (not just because the concept will appear on a test). It is obvious that the teacher has planned the lesson content well, because each lesson activity is likely to lead students to a deeper and more complete understanding of the critical concepts. Throughout the lesson, the teacher monitors and adjusts teaching to maximize the likelihood that all students achieve mastery. By the end of the lesson, the teacher knows which students have achieved the lesson objective and which students have not. Additionally, the teacher understands why some students have not yet mastered the objective and what those students need to understand in order to achieve mastery.

What It Isn't: Posting an Objective

The teacher treats the posting of the lesson objective as a routine with minimal meaning. For example, the teacher posts the objective for the day's lesson prominently in the classroom. At the beginning of the lesson, the teacher asks a student to read the objective. Once the objective is read, the teacher proceeds with lesson activities that may or may not be directly related to the lesson objective. The objective is not referenced again. At the end of the lesson, it is difficult to know what (if anything) students have learned related to the objective. It is hard to determine what was gained (other than compliance with an administrator's request) by posting the lesson objective.

* * *

What It Is: Seeking and Using Student Feedback

Continuously, the teacher seeks feedback from students regarding their understanding of critical lesson objectives. The teacher uses multiple strategies (including questions directed to individual students, group-response questions, structured discussions or debates, short written responses, performance tasks, etc.) to acquire evidence that students understand. The teacher rarely speaks for more than three minutes without asking a series of questions to ascertain what students think, what they understand, or how they understand critical concepts associated with the lesson. The teacher seeks feedback from all or almost all students (not just a few), because the teacher wants evidence of each student's level of mastery. When students respond orally, the teacher listens intently, sometimes making notes about what students understand or don't understand. When students are writing responses or completing other performance tasks, the teacher circulates among students, observing their work and commenting. Based on the feedback acquired from students, the teacher makes on-the-spot adjustments in the lesson design to maximize student understanding.

What It Isn't: Assuming Student Understanding

The teacher makes long presentations of material (through lectures, PowerPoint presentations, movies, etc.) and then asks the entire class, "Any questions?" If students don't ask questions, the teacher assumes that students understand the material. Alternately, the teacher asks specific questions and students raise their hands to be called upon. The teacher calls upon two or three students, affirms their responses, and assumes that other students understand the content. When students are asked to complete writing tasks or other performance tasks, the teacher uses the time to grade papers or manage other classroom tasks.

* * *

What It Is: Planning Lesson for the Students to be Served

The teacher plans the lesson in a way that focuses on the specific, challenging objective students need to master, while considering the students' interests, backgrounds, cultures, and prior knowledge. The teacher recognizes that textbooks and worksheets are rarely designed to tap into the motivations of diverse groups of twenty-first-century students, so activities, examples, and resources are planned that students are likely to perceive as relevant, interesting, meaningful, and fun. Many learning activities are structured into projects that challenge and stimulate students. The projects require students to apply knowledge and skills in meaningful ways that maximize student motivation and increase the likelihood that students will remember key concepts. The teacher makes foreign content feel familiar to students as they see connections to their experiences and interests. The teacher maximizes student engagement by creating learning activities that students perceive as relevant to their current lives and/or their futures.

What It Isn't: Planning Lessons for Teacher Convenience

The teacher asks students to read the lesson content from a chapter of the textbook. The chapter provides little that students perceive as relating to their interests, backgrounds, culture, or prior knowledge. After the students read the chapter, the teacher asks students to write answers to the questions that appear at the chapter's conclusion. Students do not understand why they are spending time learning the lesson content, apart from the reason they frequently hear, "It will be on the test."

* * *

What It Is: Developing Climates Where Students Feel Valued and Capable

The classroom climate leads students to perceive that the teacher cares about them. The atmosphere is calm and inviting, yet academically focused. The physical environment is attractive, featuring an abundance of high-quality student work. Students feel intellectually challenged; however, they are comfortable taking risks because they believe their teacher will help them succeed. Students are confident that their teacher will not lead them to feel humiliated. The teacher interacts with students respectfully at all times. Students feel acknowledged and appreciated for their attendance, effort, engagement, and academic progress. Students believe that the classroom is deliberately structured to ensure their learning and success.

What It Isn't: Developing Climates Where Students Feel Oppressed

The classroom is quiet. Only the most academically talented and ambitious students respond to the teacher's occasional questions. Most students are not willing to take the risk of being embarrassed. The physical environment is dull and dingy, and student work artifacts are not displayed. The teacher appears annoyed or frustrated when students ask questions, so it is not surprising that students ask very few questions. When students do not follow the teacher's specific directions, the teacher yells or responds in a tense, angry voice. Students perceive that the teacher would prefer it if they were not present. So many students sit quietly and try to disappear.

* * *

What It Is: Planning to Ensure Student Learning

In collaboration meetings, teachers focus on what they might do to maximize the likelihood that all students master lesson objectives. Teachers share their thinking about what instructional approaches might help ensure that students generate accurate, deep understandings. Teachers utilize their collective knowledge of their students, their shared understanding of the standards they wish to teach, their knowledge of the content, and their knowledge of research and best practices to plan instruction that engages all students and leads them to mastery.

What It Isn't: Planning to Ensure Coverage of Content

Collaboration meetings focus on identifying workbook pages, textbook pages, or supplemental materials that address the content of the objective. Teachers aim to have plenty of materials and activity to fill the allotted instructional minutes and to "cover" the objective, but teachers do not engage in detailed discussion of how they might provide instruction that leads their students to master the content.

School Self-Assessment Tool: Does Your School Provide Effective Instruction that Results in Engagement and Mastery?

This self-assessment will help you determine the extent to which your school provides effective instruction for all students. Consider working with a team of teachers, administrators, parents, and students to respond to these questions. (One could invite participants to provide individual ratings.) Completion of the self-assessment will generate a picture of the school's current practices. By utilizing the same process annually or semi-annually, the school can assess progress toward developing effective instruction for all students. Rate the following on a scale of 1 to 5, with 1 representing NOT LIKELY and 5 representing VERY LIKELY.

I. How likely is it that every lesson taught in your school is designed to ensure that all students served will demonstrate mastery of specific learning objective? Rating _____

If the rating varies, explain to what extent it varies and why: _____
_____

a. How likely is it that the students your school serves perceive that all learning objectives are clear and meaningful? Rating _____

If the rating varies, explain to what extent it varies and why: _____
_____

b. How likely is it that all learning activities within each lesson align to the objective for the lesson? Rating _____

If the rating varies, explain to what extent it varies and why: _____
_____

c. How likely is it that, during each lesson taught, the teacher seeks evidence about the extent to which students are making progress toward mastering the objective? Rating _____

If the rating varies, explain to what extent it varies and why: _____
_____

d. How likely is it that the presentation of each lesson's content is sufficiently clear, logical, and concise to result in students achieving mastery? Rating _____

If the rating varies, explain to what extent it varies and why: _____
_____

II. How likely is it that the diverse groups of students served at your school will engage actively in academic lessons? Rating _____

If the rating varies, explain to what extent it varies and why: _____

_____

   a. How likely is it that lessons will connect with the backgrounds, cultures, interest, and prior knowledge of the diverse groups of students served? Rating _____

     If the rating varies, explain to what extent it varies and why: _____

     _____

   b. How likely is it that lessons will engage students in real dialogue that requires them to utilize the vocabulary that is essential to mastering the objective? Rating _____

     If the rating varies, explain to what extent it varies and why: _____

     _____

   c. How likely is it that the students served at your school will perceive that lessons are relevant, stimulating, and worthwhile? Rating _____

     If the rating varies, explain to what extent it varies and why: _____

     _____

III. How likely is it that the diverse groups of students served at your school perceive that they are valued, respected, and appreciated by their teachers? Rating _____

If the rating varies, explain to what extent it varies and why: _____

_____

   a. How likely is it that the diverse groups of students served at your school perceive that teachers know them individually and know some things about their lives beyond school? Rating _____

     If the rating varies, explain to what extent it varies and why: _____

     _____

   b. How likely is it that the diverse groups of students served at your school perceive that teachers value their presence, their thinking, and their effort? Rating _____

     If the rating varies, explain to what extent it varies and why: _____

     _____

IV. How likely is it that teachers at your school perceive that regular collaboration with colleagues helps them plan effective instruction that leads students to engagement and mastery? Rating _____

If the rating varies, explain to what extent it varies and why: _____

_____

V. How likely is it that teachers at your school perceive that frequent classroom observations and feedback build their capacity to provide effective instruction that leads their students to engagement and mastery? Rating _____

If the rating varies, explain to what extent it varies and why: _____
_____

VI. How likely is it that teachers at your school perceive that focused professional development builds their capacity to provide effective instruction that leads their students to engagement and mastery? Rating _____

If the rating varies, explain to what extent it varies and why: _____
_____

References

Bondy, E., & Ross, D.D. (2008). The teacher as warm demander. *Educational Leadership, 66*(1), 54–58.

Boykin, A., & Noguera, P. (2011). *Creating the opportunity to learn: Moving from research to practice to close the achievement gap.* Alexandria, VA: Association for Supervision and Curriculum Development.

Brown, B., & Saks, D. (1986). Measuring the effects of instructional time on student learning: Evidence from the beginning teacher evaluation study. *American Journal of Education, 94*(4), 480–500.

Delpit, L. (1995). *Other people's children: Cultural conflict in the classroom.* New York: The New Press.

Ferguson, R. (2002). *What doesn't meet the eye: Understanding and addressing racial disparities in high-achieving suburban schools.* Oak Brook, IL: North Central Regional Educational Lab.

Fisher, D., & Frey, N. (2007). *Checking for understanding: Formative assessment techniques for your classroom.* Alexandria, VA: Association for Supervision and Curriculum Development.

Gay, G. (2010). *Culturally responsive teaching: Theory, research, and practice*, 2nd ed. New York: Teachers College Press.

Irvine, J.J., & Fraser, J.W. (1998). Warm demanders. *Education Week, 17*(35), 56.

Kunjufu, J. (2002). *Black students, Middle class teachers.* Chicago, IL: African American Images.

Ladson-Billings, G. (1994). *The dreamkeepers: Successful teachers of African American children.* San Francisco, CA: Jossey-Bass.

Ladson-Billings, G. (2002). I ain't writin' nuttin': Permissions to fail and demands to succeed in urban classrooms. In L. Delpit & J.K. Dowdy (eds.), *The skin that we speak: Thoughts on language and culture in the classroom* (pp. 107–120). New York: The New Press.

McKenzie, K.B., & Skrla, L. (2011). *Using equity audits in the classroom to reach and teach all students.* Thousand Oaks, CA: Corwin.

National Policy Board for Educational Administration (2015). *Professional Standards for Educational Leaders*. Retrieved from Reston, VA: www.ccsso.org/Documents/2015/ProfessionalStandardsforEducationalLeaders2015forNPBEA-FINAL.pdf.

Pearson, P. D., & Gallagher, M. C. (1983). The instruction of reading comprehension. *Contemporary Educational Psychology, 8*, 317–344.

Putnam, R. T., & Borko, H. (1997). Teacher learning: Implications of new views of cognition. In B. J. Biddle, T. L. Good, & I. F. Goodson (eds.), *The international handbook of teachers and teaching* (pp. 1223–1296). Dordrecht, The Netherlands: Kluwer.

Saphier, J., Haley-Speca, M.A., & Gower, R. (2008). *The skillful teacher: Building your teaching skills*, 6th ed. [Kindle] Acton, MA: Research for Better Teaching, Inc.

Tschannen-Moran, M., Uline, C., Hoy, A., & Mackley, T. (2000). Creating smarter schools through collaboration. *Journal of Educational Administration*, *38*(3), 247–272.

Part II

Leadership that Promotes Outstanding Results for All Students

Leading schools to become places where all demographic groups of students 1) benefit from a positive transformational culture, 2) have access to challenging academic curricula, and 3) receive effective instruction that results in engagement and mastery is not easy. Fiscal resources are important, but are clearly not sufficient. A report by Stanford researchers indicated that some of the nation's largest achievement gaps are found in some of the wealthiest districts (Sparks, 2016). Many of these wealthy districts boast about their well-paid and highly qualified teachers and principals; however, they do not come close to generating equitable learning outcomes for the diverse groups of students they serve.

Chapters 2, 3, and 4 described the characteristics of schools that achieve excellent and equitable learning results. As well, the chapters described the elements of the coherent educational improvement system that helped the schools nurture these characteristics across classrooms, grade levels, and disciplines. Our studies of high-performing urban schools suggest that leaders are not likely to achieve widespread, sustainable evidence of excellent and equitable learning results without developing these school-wide characteristics. As well, success is unlikely without the development of a coherent educational improvement system designed to achieve each of the five outcomes articulated in Chapter 1.

Additionally, we believe our readers need to understand the day-to-day leadership challenges that influence whether or not schools escape the quagmires that characterize so many urban schools. Orr, Byrne-Jimenez, McFarlane, and Brown (2005) observed: "an implicit assumption in the leadership literature that the urban principalship is similar to all principalships in all contexts, albeit with fewer resources, greater demands to attend to students' personal and social problems, and more complicated political dynamics" (p. 24). Instead, "the challenges facing leaders of inner-city schools are typically quite different from those facing leaders of schools in the leafy suburbs . . . [and these] unique contexts . . . require unique enactments of successful leadership" (Leithwood, Harris, & Strauss, 2010, pp. 17, 19). Put simply, even the most energetic, creative, and ambitious leaders cannot lead a school to excellent and equitable learning results without the effort of many others, including teachers, counselors, secretaries, custodians, nurses, administrators (both school-level and district-level administrators), parents/family members, community-agency staff, and students. School leaders, working solo, will not be able to establish the school characteristics or improvement systems necessary to transform their schools. Urban school leaders will not generate excellent and equitable learning results unless they influence a critical mass of the school community members. In particular, leaders face the following four major challenges that influence their ability to make any significant progress:

1) Leaders must build within their faculty, staff, parents, and students a desire to change culture, curricula, and instruction. Leaders must help everyone generate a compelling answer to the question, "*Why* should we invest the effort required to change?" (This challenge is discussed in Chapter 5.)

2) Leaders must build within their faculty, staff, parents, and students a belief that desired changes in culture, curricula, and instruction can be achieved at their school and within their areas of work and responsibility. Leaders must help everyone generate a common answer to the question, "*Why not* now? *Why not* here? Do we not possess whatever is necessary to make progress toward the desired change?" (This challenge is discussed in Chapter 6.)

3) Leaders must build within their faculty, staff, parents, and students a clear understanding of their roles and responsibilities related to essential changes in culture, curricula, and instruction. Leaders must help everyone generate answers to the question, "*What* is my role? *What* are the few critical things I must do in order to contribute to the desired change?" (This challenge is discussed in Chapter 7.)

4) Leaders must build within their faculty, staff, parents, and students a belief that they have the capacity, support, and resources necessary to implement essential changes in culture, curricula, and instruction. Leaders must help everyone generate a common answer to the question, "*How* can I provide the individuals I support (my faculty, staff, parents, students, and/or children) what they need in order to progress toward the desired change?" (This challenge is discussed in Chapter 8.)

These challenges vary in intensity across different schools and districts. In some cases, the challenges vary within schools, as different groups pose different concerns that threaten the leader's vision of change. So, leaders must be aware of all four of these challenges, and they must be prepared to address them effectively.

References

Leithwood, K., Louis, K.S., Anderson, S., & Wahlstrom, K. (2004). *Review of research: How leadership influences student learning.* New York: The Wallace Foundation.

Orr, T.M., Byrne-Jimenez, M., McFarlane, P., & Brown, B. (2005). Leading out from low-performing schools: The urban principal experience. *Leadership and Policy in Schools, 4/1*, 23–54, DOI: 10.1080/15700760590924609.

Sparks, S.D. (May 11, 2016). Rich districts post widest racial gaps: Database sheds new light on achievement disparities. *Education Week, 35*(30), 1, 12.

Leadership that Influences the Desire to Change

5

The teachers have common planning, so they meet every day in the war room and we discuss data. We don't only talk about end-of-course data, but we talk about SAT and ACT and we keep track of all our students. We highlight where everyone is. What are we doing? What do the students need? Do we need to call parents? We also look at attendance. Our goal is 96 percent average daily attendance . . .

One of the questions posed to us is, "Why the war room? Why not the situation room? Why not this? Why not that?" When our military goes to battle, there's a room that they call the war room. In that room, they strategize and come up with ideas. "We're going to come in from this side. We're going to come in from that side." They come up with their interventions and that's exactly what we do in that room with our teachers. We're in a war. We're in a battle for the education of each individual child. The ultimate goal is to get them to graduate. And together, along with the teacher, that's what we're doing. We're winning—one goal, one mind, one child at a time.

Rose Longoria, Principal, James Pace Early College
High School, Brownsville, TX

It's all about leadership. She [the principal] came in here with a vision and the rest of us followed suit. She came with a vision. She changed patterns, she changed mentalities, and she changed perceptions. Students started buying into it. Teachers started buying into it. They started being proud of it.

Obed Leal, Early College Director/Assistant Principal,
James Pace Early College High School, Brownsville, TX

Having a great vision is essential, but not sufficient. Leaders must also help everyone who plays a role in accomplishing the vision see the vision as appealing and worth the requisite effort.

This chapter focuses upon the first of the leadership challenges: building the desire to change. One might think that anyone would be eager to embrace an effort likely to reduce the frustration and despair found in some urban schools. There are, however, many school leaders who could describe disturbing situations in which teachers, support staff, administrators, and even parents and students resisted, sabotaged, or fought aggressively against change efforts that promised to bring superior results. Muhammad (2009) explained that people resist change when they are not provided with a clear rationale. Many leaders fail to enact change when stakeholders do not perceive a compelling reason to engage in the hard work of changing ineffective and sometimes counterproductive behaviors, routines, or practices. Often leaders fail to offer a compelling "why."

Table 5.1. Common Reasons for Change and Common Responses

Typical Schools

Common Reasons Offered by Leaders for Why Change is Essential	Common Responses from School Personnel	Common Responses from Parents and Students
We have to improve student test scores.	"Test scores aren't a real measure of what's important." "We care about student learning, not test scores."	"They're just looking for more ways to prove that we're failures." "Those tests were created for middle-class kids. Our kids were never intended to succeed on those tests." "I'm probably going to end up dropping out just like my older brothers. Why should I worry about test scores?"
We need to change in order to meet federal and/or state mandates.	"The state has been threatening this school for years and nothing happens because they don't care about these kids." "If the state chooses to do anything, it will likely be you [the principal] who gets fired. We'll be fine because we have a contract." "I didn't become a teacher because I wanted to achieve AYP."	"The state doesn't care about our community. Why should we care about what the state wants?" "Who cares how the state rates this school? Everybody already knows it's a lousy school."
The superintendent expects us to accomplish this.	"We'll have a new superintendent again in a year and a half and this will be forgotten." "The superintendent doesn't even know where this school is. She certainly doesn't know what our kids need."	"The superintendent doesn't care about our community. The school board only cares at election time."
This proposed change is research based.	"The researchers never met our kids and our parents. It probably worked in some affluent suburban school with abundant resources." "Nothing ever works at this school."	"How could researchers know what would be best for our children and our community?"

Table 5.1. **(Continued)**

Typical Schools

Common Reasons Offered by Leaders for Why Change is Essential	Common Responses from School Personnel	Common Responses from Parents and Students
You need to do this because I am the principal.	*"That's what the last principal said, and the principal before him, and the principal before her. They're all gone and we're still here."*	*"The principal just wants us to make her look good so she can get a better job in the suburbs."*

Table 5.1 shares a list of reasons leaders in typical urban schools utilize to encourage changes in behavior, programs, or systems. As well, the list includes some of the spoken or unspoken stakeholder responses that suggest leaders have failed to influence the desire to change.

As we have endeavored to coach and support leaders in many typical urban schools, we have seen leaders, overtly and covertly, put forth these reasons for action. As well, we have heard these and similar responses from many stakeholders.

Stakeholders need to believe that they are being asked to change their practice for a worthwhile reason. In high-performing schools, leaders articulated and regularly reinforced noble reasons for change. For example, at James Pace Early College High School in Brownsville, Texas, administrators emphasized that they were "in a battle for the education of each individual child." As the quote at the beginning of this chapter illustrates, administrators sought to help school personnel see a vision in which they were "winning—one goal, one mind, one child at a time."

The importance of the leader's vision has been described extensively (Cotton, 2003; Hallinger & Heck, 1996; Leithwood, Louis, Anderson, & Walhstrom, 2004; Murphy & Torre, 2015). These studies emphasize, and our studies of high-performing urban schools confirm, that leaders must not only have a vision of a desired state, but they must also lead others to share that same vision. Leaders in very high-performing urban schools succeeded in getting a critical mass of stakeholders (teachers, support staff, administrators, parents, and students) to see and desire a vision of educational excellence and equity: a vision that included a positive transformational culture, challenging academic curricula, and effective instruction that will lead all students to high levels of engagement and mastery.

In order to lead their schools to attain strong learning results for every demographic group, leaders must influence a critical mass of stakeholders to rally behind a powerful reason for change. None of the leaders we interviewed claimed that they had succeeded in getting every stakeholder to modify practices, routines, or structures in the ways they hoped; however, the leaders had clearly convinced a sufficient number of stakeholders to do so, thus building the necessary momentum for change. In each high-performing urban school, it was easy to find large groups of teachers, parents, and students who spoke proudly about the direction their school had taken and the vision for excellence that motivated their efforts.

Having a great vision is essential, but not sufficient. Leaders must also help everyone who plays a role in accomplishing the vision see the vision as appealing and worth the requisite effort. Leaders in the high-performing schools we studied framed reasons for change that resonated with various stakeholders.

Framing a Reason for Change that Resonates

A principal related the story of his initial efforts to engage his teachers in reform efforts. The principal explained to teachers that changes were necessary to ensure that the school met federal and state AYP (Adequate Yearly Progress) requirements. The principal reported that one teacher loudly spoke up for several by exclaiming, "We didn't become teachers because we wanted to improve test scores and we didn't become teachers because we wanted to meet AYP! We became teachers because we wanted to help children."

Often leaders have the right goal at heart, but they fail to present the goal in a way that resonates with key stakeholders (the individuals and groups essential to the successful pursuit of the goal). Teachers, parents, students, and community members have been known to demonize leaders who frame the desired change in a way that fails to resonate with their values. Too often, individuals perceive that their leaders propose changes to comply with policy mandates.

Blankstein and Noguera (2015) insisted that successful leaders overcame opposition by emphasizing the moral imperative for change. They wrote:

> While some comply with equity mandates as a result of external pressure or desegregation orders, we would argue that the courageous action and leadership that is required to enact excellence through equity can only be *sustained* if they are grounded in clear and unflinching moral reasoning. (p. 9)

In the high-performing urban schools studied, leaders listened to colleagues, parents, community members, and students and then framed the reason for essential changes in ways that would resonate with them, generally because of the moral imperative associated with the proposed goal. So, the leaders used the goal as a rallying point. For example, at Horace Mann Elementary in Glendale, California, the goal of getting every child to achieve proficiency in literacy became a rallying point for change. At Kearny School of International Business in San Diego, the compelling goal was to see every student graduate from high school while simultaneously acquiring college credits.

In some cases, specific language might influence how stakeholders respond to a reason or purpose for action. When leaders have engaged in adequate conversation with individuals and small groups of stakeholders, prior to publicly articulating the reasons for a change, leaders have a better chance of avoiding language that triggers negative responses. For example, strong emphasis on the state accountability system might stir a negative response in a school where teachers and other school personnel perceive that the accountability system is unfair and underestimates the accomplishments of their students. If the people with primary responsibility for enacting the change do not value the articulated purpose of the change, the desired change may never happen.

In many of the high-performing schools, leaders recognized that stakeholders were motivated by a desire to make a substantial difference in the lives of the students they served. Several principals noted, as did the principal of Cecil H. Parker

Elementary in Mount Vernon, New York, that the professionals, paraprofessionals, and volunteers who worked with them "came to work here, because they really wanted to do something special in the lives of children." Leaders listened to those sentiments and tried to frame the reasons for change efforts accordingly.

Leaders in the high-performing urban schools seemed to understand (perhaps intrinsically) that stakeholders would not be motivated to engage in the hard work of changing practices simply for the purpose of achieving mediocrity. As Magdalena Aguilar, the former principal of Escontrias Elementary in El Paso's Socorro Independent School District explained, "People aren't going to work as hard as they do here if they believe that the prize is just an Acceptable state rating." Similarly, an administrator at Lawndale High School in Los Angeles stated:

> If people think that the goal is just to increase our performance by a few percentage points, they will think that it's OK if a lot of students drop out of school, or if a lot of our students are not prepared for college. And that's not OK. People here are proud that they are doing something special for kids. They know that they make a difference: a big difference for kids.

Leaders successfully initiated coherent educational improvement systems because they were able to convince a critical mass of stakeholders that the envisioned change was worth their effort. In fact, leaders were able to create environments in which stakeholders felt ownership of the vision. For example, Manriquez (2012) reported in her study of a high-performing urban high school that when the principal started the small school, about half of the teachers seemed committed to the vision of getting all of their students prepared to succeed in college (the vision espoused by the principal). The other half had been placed at the school based on seniority rights or other district decisions. The faculty members committed to constructive change proved to be a critical mass, because they were vocal, assertive, and determined to make a positive difference. The principal supported and nurtured those teacher leaders so that, together, they established the positive, transformational culture that drove change throughout the school.

Manriquez (2012) described the principal's account of a staff meeting that illustrated the way in which the critical mass not only influenced the impetus for change, but also helped to sustain the momentum:

> I remember our second meeting during a school year, and a teacher who was placed here because she was displaced [from another school] started complaining about the reading scores and how low our kids were reading. And [she complained about] how the parents weren't participating, and blah, blah, blah, you know the typical, "everything is horrible." And one of my teachers, just in the middle of the meeting (and there were like 25 of us) stands up and looks at her and says, "You know what, we are not a culture of complaint. We are not doing this. We are not going backward." And I did not have to say anything. (p. 72)

The teachers had become the keepers of the vision. They resisted when others tried to derail the school's momentum.

Specifying Who Will Benefit from the Change

While each high-performing urban school might have emphasized different details as it framed reasons for change, they all shared surprising consistency and impressive clarity as they emphasized that change efforts were intended to benefit all students. Leaders made extra efforts to clarify that the proposed efforts to change culture, curriculum, and instruction would substantially benefit each and every student served.

Fullan (2006) emphasized that the first of 10 key elements for turning around schools was to define closing gaps as the overarching goal. He explained:

> Raising the bar and closing the gap, as we have seen, is not just a slogan. It captures a host of issues that go to the very core of how a society functions. The first thing is to realize that decreasing the gap between high and low performers—boys, girls, ethnic groups, poor, rich, special education—is crucial because it has so many social consequences. The remaining nine strategic focuses are all in the service of gap closing. (p. 45)

Leaders in the high-performing urban schools studied made sure that stakeholders perceived that the purpose behind change efforts was to benefit all of the students, not just certain groups of students. Leaders recognized that a noble vision could meet quick resistance if stakeholders believed that some groups of students would not benefit substantially from the efforts. So, even though high-performing urban schools gave special attention to groups of students with greater needs (e.g., students with disabilities, English learners, students who were not on track to earn sufficient credits to graduate, Black students, Latino students, male students, or any of several other groups), the overarching purpose of improvement efforts emphasized a focus on all students. These schools achieved excellent and equitable learning results because excellence and equity were explicit reasons for the effort.

Simultaneously, leaders made it clear that proposed changes were not intended to benefit the principal or other administrators. Repeatedly we heard principals say, "It's not about me. It's about the students." Even when the change might have satisfied a district administrator, or made life easier for the principal, school leaders underscored the benefit to students. Chenoweth (2007) emphasized that, in the high-performing schools she studied, "They made decisions on what is good for kids, not what is good for adults" (p. 219). To the greatest extent possible, leaders avoided using coercion or authoritarian power to move people to act. Instead, they appealed to the moral commitments of stakeholders and helped people see how a proposed action would be of substantial benefit to students.

For example, teachers at several of the high-performing urban schools reported that it had been difficult to move to regular teacher collaboration routines when they had not been accustomed to working or planning together. A teacher at Escontrias Elementary in the Socorro Independent School District explained how the principal helped teachers embrace teacher collaboration opportunities:

> She [the principal] was so good at explaining how this [collaboration] would help us help our students. She made it seem like any reasonable, caring human being would want to do this. So, yes, I suppose we had to participate. But, we really did it because she convinced us that it was just the right thing to do for our students.

As leaders continuously emphasize how students benefit from changes in teacher work routines, they create the conditions for developing new norms of collective responsibility (Louis, Marks, & Kruse, 1996). Teachers begin to hold themselves and each other accountable for student learning, embracing their common purpose in improving instruction for every child. Conversely, principals who emphasize "Do it, because I said so" are more likely to encounter subtle resistance, outright rebellion, or token compliance. ("I'll sit there for the required minutes and I'll write the minimum he expects on the form, but I won't do more than that and I won't let it change anything about my teaching.")

It is important to note that many principals acknowledged there were times when they felt compelled to resort to their positional authority as administrators. For example, principals reported times when they sanctioned, disciplined, or removed teachers from their positions. It is fascinating, however, that teachers rarely, if ever, mentioned those actions. Instead, teachers reported that their principals were student-centered, positive, and focused on supporting everyone's success.

Basing Every Decision on the Fundamental Reason for Change

Developing a high-performing urban school is like running a marathon. Helping distance runners achieve a great start might be helpful, but could also be meaningless without consistent attention to conditioning, breathing, running technique, and strategy. Moving stakeholders to internalize a compelling reason for change may be helpful, but could be meaningless if the rationale blurs or disappears in the day-to-day routines and decisions that occur in the school. Leaders in the high-performing schools studied accomplished ambitious changes in culture, curriculum, and instruction, in part, because they demonstrated consistency and persistence. They kept stakeholders ever mindful of the reasons for day-to-day decisions. They maintained a laser focus on students, never giving stakeholders reasons to believe that other priorities influenced decisions or expectations.

At James Pace Early College High School in Brownsville, Texas, the principal and the entire school leadership team kept the focus on "the battle for the education of each individual child." Constantly, they asked, "What needs to be done to help this student? What can I [the administrator] do to help? How long has it been since someone talked with the parent? What can we do to get this student to succeed?" Teachers, support staff, students, and parents perceived the consistency as evidence of sincerity. In particular, one teacher commented, "Our administrators really believe that we can get each one of these kids to succeed, graduate, and go on to have a productive life. It's what they're all about. It's what this school is all about."

Similarly, leaders in other high-performing urban schools consistently emphasized the student-focused reasons for actions. At schools like Branch Brook Elementary in Newark, New Jersey; Horace Mann Elementary in Glendale, California; and Maplewood Richmond Heights High School in St. Louis, Missouri, principals told students repeatedly that lofty expectations for student work (especially student writing) were an expression of the school's commitment to their future success. At schools like Dr. Charles T. Lunsford School in Rochester, New York; William Dandy Middle School in Fort Lauderdale, Florida; or Golden Empire Elementary in Sacramento, California, principals helped parents understand that ambitious expectations for student work were designed to ensure their children's current and future academic success. Whenever leaders at any of the high-performing schools asked teachers to assume new tasks or roles, they clearly explained how the additional effort would be of great benefit to their students.

Leaders were able to influence higher levels of effort and commitment from students, parents, and school employees, in part, because they inspired trust. Tschannen-Moran (2014) explained that five facets influenced the development of trust: benevolence, honesty, openness, reliability, and competence. By articulating a consistent authentic commitment to the best interest of students, leaders demonstrated benevolence. Their honesty, openness, and consistency about the reasons for their decisions also helped stakeholders trust that the leader had sincere, worthwhile intentions. In the absence of trust, it is unlikely that the schools would have developed coherent educational improvement systems or the empowering school characteristics described in Chapters 2, 3, and 4.

Summary

Leaders in the high-performing urban schools nurtured a sense of purpose, a sense of mission. This is not in reference to the mission statement on the wall. It is, instead, related to a sense of mission that lives in the hearts of all members of the school community.

Meaningful school improvement requires stakeholders (including students, parents, and school employees) to work differently. Generally, human beings need compelling reasons to step beyond their comfort zones and work differently. Often, leaders incorrectly assume that stakeholders will be compelled to act by the same concerns that compelled them to act. Also, some leaders incorrectly assume that they can make people change simply by exercising their positional power. In high-performing urban schools, leaders help ensure that everyone understands why change is important. They help people perceive a powerful purpose for the substantial work of school improvement. Leaders in the high-performing urban schools nurtured a sense of purpose, a sense of mission. This is not in reference to the mission statement on the wall. It is, instead, related to a sense of mission that lives in the hearts of all members of the school community.

Deal and Peterson (2009) described the importance of this sense of purpose and mission when they wrote:

> At the hub of a school's culture are its mission and purpose—the revered focus of what people do. Although not easy to define, mission and purpose trigger intangible forces that inspire teachers to teach, school leaders to lead, children to learn, and parents and the community to have confidence and faith in their school. (p. 61)

In the high-performing urban schools studied, leaders framed reasons for change in ways that resonated with the various stakeholders they served. Leaders listened to the concerns of students, parents, and school employees and framed the purpose of change efforts accordingly. In particular, leaders emphasized that a key purpose of change was to benefit students. Leaders kept students at the fore and minimized the extent to which individuals and groups might think that the proposed changes simply served the principal's needs.

Beyond initial efforts to frame the reasons for change, leaders in high-performing urban schools regularly reinforced the reasons for change efforts. With each new decision and each new expectation, leaders reminded stakeholders of the compelling reason for seeking improvements. In each case, leaders emphasized the impact on students' lives. This benevolence, openness, honesty, and consistency inspired increasing levels of trust. Over time, stakeholders expressed an increased willingness to engage in the hard work associated with improving culture, curricula, and instruction.

What It Is & What It Isn't: Leadership that Influences the Desire to Change

What It Is: Advancing the Perception that the School Is Pursuing the Right Goals

As school leaders communicate the reasons for their decisions, actions, and expectations they clearly articulate a rationale that resonates with the school's various stakeholder groups (students, parents, community members, school employees). Leaders are careful about framing their language in a manner that is sensitive to the concerns and experiences of local stakeholders. When leaders describe the purpose for change efforts, stakeholders respond positively because they perceive that the school is pursuing the right goals.

What It Isn't: Advancing the Perception that the School Is Focused on Compliance

School leaders do not discuss the reasons for the change efforts they advance, because they assume that the reasons are obvious. They couch goals in terms related to accountability systems and federal, state, and district mandates, and they assume that teachers, parents, and students will appreciate the rationale for those goals.

*   *   *

What It Is: Focusing on All Students

Leaders elevate discussions about change efforts by focusing on the impact to students. Leaders help stakeholders believe that if they pursue the change efforts, together they will make a positive difference in the lives of students. Even when some change efforts might provide more immediate benefits to specific groups of students, leaders emphasize how changes will help all students. As a result, the harshest critics have a difficult time arguing against the spirit that underlies improvement efforts.

What It Isn't: Enabling Perceptions of Power Games

Stakeholders tend to make guesses about who is served by the changes they are asked to enact. They presume that the real benefactors are administrators who win power struggles each time they succeed at getting other stakeholders to pursue a different course of action.

*   *   *

What It Is: Continuously Reinforcing Messages about Rationale

School leaders continuously remind stakeholders about why they are engaging in improvement efforts. Reminders are often tied to praise and words of appreciation as administrators make comments such as, "The time you're investing in doing this is really going to make a difference for your students when they get to the next grade." School personnel, parents, and students are more likely to invest sincere effort because they believe that they are contributing toward important outcomes.

What It Isn't: Sporadically/Inconsistently Communicating about Rationale

The principal speaks eloquently about the reasons for proposed changes at beginning-of-the-year events, but rarely mentions the reasons for the changes afterward. Stakeholders forget why they are being asked to engage in such hard work. Administrative decisions throughout the year seem disconnected to the rationale discussed at year-opening events.

School Self-Assessment Tool: Does Your School Leadership Positively Influence the Desire to Change?

This self-assessment will help you determine the extent to which leadership at your school influences the desire to change. Consider engaging teams of teachers, administrators, parents, and students to respond to these questions. (One could invite participants to provide individual ratings and then compile separate ratings for stakeholder groups.) Completion of the self-assessment will generate a picture of the school's current practices. By utilizing the same process annually or semi-annually, the school community can assess progress in influencing the desire to change. Rate the following on a scale of 1 to 5, with 1 representing NOT LIKELY and 5 representing VERY LIKELY.

I. How likely is it that students (including all demographic groups of students) perceive that they are being asked to work harder/smarter for reasons that are focused on their wellbeing? Rating _____

If different demographic groups of students would be likely to respond to this item differently, explain to what extent responses would vary and why: _____

_____

II. When school leaders ask students to assume new tasks, meet higher expectations, or work harder or smarter, how likely is it that leaders offer students reasons that inspire students to exert maximum effort? Rating _____

If the answer to this item might differ when considering different demographic groups of students, explain to what extent responses would vary and why: _____

_____

III. When school leaders ask students to assume new tasks, meet higher expectations, or work harder or smarter, how likely is it that students perceive that the reasons for the requests are primarily focused on the needs of school personnel? Rating _____

If the answer to this item might differ when considering different demographic groups of students, explain to what extent responses would vary and why: _____

IV. To what extent are students likely to perceive that all administrative decisions regarding expectations, policies, and programs consistently reflect the purposes and rationale that school leaders articulate? Rating _____

If the answer to this item might differ when considering different demographic groups of students, explain to what extent responses would vary and why: _____

V. How likely is it that parents (including parents of all demographic groups of students) perceive that they are being asked to work harder/smarter for reasons that are focused on their children's wellbeing? Rating _____

If different groups of parents would be likely to respond to this item differently, explain to what extent responses would vary and why: _____

VI. When school leaders ask parents to assume new tasks, meet higher expectations, or work harder or smarter, how likely is it that leaders offer parents reasons that inspire parents to exert maximum effort? Rating _____

If the answer to this item might differ when considering different demographic groups of parents, explain to what extent responses would vary and why: _____

VII. When school leaders ask parents to assume new tasks, meet higher expectations, or work harder or smarter, how likely is it that parents perceive that the reasons for the requests are primarily focused on the needs of school personnel? Rating _____

If the answer to this item might differ when considering different demographic groups of parents, explain to what extent responses would vary and why: _____

VIII. To what extent are parents likely to perceive that all administrative decisions regarding expectations, policies, and programs consistently reflect the purposes and rationale that school leaders articulate? Rating _____

If the answer to this item might differ when considering different demographic groups of parents, explain to what extent responses would vary and why: _____

IX. How likely is it that school personnel (including different groups of school personnel such as teachers, counselors, custodians, etc.) perceive that they are being asked to work harder/smarter for reasons that are focused on the wellbeing of students? Rating _____

If different school personnel groups would be likely to respond to this item differently, explain to what extent responses would vary and why: _____

X. When school leaders ask school personnel to assume new tasks, meet higher expectations, or work harder or smarter, how likely is it that leaders offer school personnel reasons that inspire students to exert maximum effort? Rating _____

If the answer to this item might differ when considering different groups of school personnel, explain to what extent responses would vary and why: _____

XI. When school leaders ask school personnel to assume new tasks, meet higher expectations, or work harder or smarter, how likely is it that school personnel perceive that the reasons for the requests are primarily focused on the needs of administrators? Rating _____

If the answer to this item might differ when considering different groups of school personnel, explain to what extent responses would vary and why: _____

XII. To what extent are school personnel likely to perceive that all administrative decisions regarding expectations, policies, and programs consistently reflect the purposes and rationale that school leaders articulate? Rating _____

If the answer to this item might differ when considering different groups of school personnel, explain to what extent responses would vary and why: _____

References

Blankstein, A.M., & Noguera, P. (2015). *Excellence through equity: Five principles of courageous leadership to guide achievement for every student.* Thousand Oaks, CA: Corwin.

Chenoweth, K. (2007). *It's being done: Academic success in unexpected schools.* Cambridge, MA: Harvard Education Press.

Cotton, K. (2003). *Principals and student achievement: What the research says.* Arlington, VA: Association for Supervision and Curriculum Development.

Deal, T. E., & Peterson, K. D. (2009). *Shaping school culture: Pitfalls, paradoxes, and promises,* 2nd ed. San Francisco, CA: John Wiley & Sons, Inc.

Fullan, M. (2006). *Turnaround leadership.* San Francisco, CA: Jossey-Bass.

Hallinger, P., & Heck, R. (1996). Reassessing the principal's role in school effectiveness: A review of empirical research, 1980–1995. *Educational Administration Quarterly, 32*(1), 5–44.

Leithwood, K., Harris, A., & Strauss, T. (2010). *Leading school turnaround: How successful leaders transform low-performing schools.* San Francisco, CA: John Wiley and Sons, Inc.

Leithwood, K., Louis, K.S., Anderson, S., & Wahlstrom, K. (2004). *Review of research: How leadership influences student learning.* New York: The Wallace Foundation.

Louis, K.S., Marks, H.M., & Kruse, S. (1996). Teachers' professional community in restructuring schools. *American Educational Research Journal, 33,* 757–798.

Manriquez, C. (2012). *Turnaround schools: A comparative case study of two small schools.* D.Ed. dissertation, San Diego State University.

Muhammad, A. (2009). *Transforming school culture: How to overcome staff division.* Bloomington, IN: Solution Tree Press.

Murphy, J., & Torre, D. (2015). Vision: Essential scaffolding. *Educational Management Administration and Leadership, 43*(2), 177–197.

Tschannen-Moran, M. (2014). *Trust matters: Leadership in successful schools*, 2nd ed. San Francisco, CA: Jossey-Bass.

6 Leadership that Influences Belief in the Capacity to Improve and Succeed

Why do we work so hard? Well, you know that most of us kids went to other high schools around here and we were kicked out or suspended or other stuff happened. At my old school, the teachers would see me coming and think, "Here comes trouble. Here comes a headache. Here comes my next suspension. Here comes a dropout." They saw me as another Black statistic. Even though I knew I wasn't stupid, I pretty much figured they were right. I was never good at school. I had a hard time reading the textbooks. I just didn't see how I was going to get anywhere at school or in life.

So when I came here, I thought it would be all about hanging with my friends. But then, when I got here, the teachers saw me differently. They looked at me like, "Here comes potential. Here comes a future graduate. Here comes a future college student." That's the way they treated me. That's the way they talk to all of us. So, when you're treated that way, it just makes everything different. You want to work hard because you want them [the adults] to be right about you. You don't want them to change their minds.

So, even when we're allowed to go back to our other schools, almost all of us stay here. I'm going to graduate from this school. Then, I'm going on to college.

Eleventh-grade student, Dayton Business
Technology High School, Dayton, OH

Yes, working at this school is hard, but we love it. We know that, as a team, we make all the difference in kids' lives. We couldn't do it if we worked as individuals, but as a team, we're impressive. Our principal is one of us. She believes in us and we believe in each other. That makes it so much easier for us to believe in our kids. It makes it easier to get up in the morning and drive downtown and be excited for this opportunity each day. Do you know that 59 per cent of our students go on to college? That may not seem like much for a typical high school, but that's pretty amazing here. Probably fewer than five percent would have said they were going to college a week before they entered this school. We work hard because we see the difference we're making.

Teacher, Dayton Business Technology
High School, Dayton, OH

To establish a positive transformational culture, challenging curricula, and effective instruction that lead to excellent and equitable learning results, stakeholders need to believe that their efforts will not be in vain. Students need to believe that their struggles to comprehend and excel will not lead to more failure experiences. In many cases, parents need to believe that their children have a greater chance for school success than they experienced when they were students. Teachers need to believe that school leaders are not setting them up for frustration and failure. Even if stakeholders perceive that the leader is pursuing the right goal, they are not likely to exert maximum effort if they do not perceive a reasonable chance of success. The students at Dayton Business Technology High School believed that their teachers knew that they had the ability to succeed in life, even when the students had experienced serious academic and behavioral challenges. A teacher at Morris Slingluff Elementary in Dothan, Alabama explained, "The children believe that we believe in them." At Morris Slingluff, at Dayton Business Technology High School, and at the other high-performing urban schools we studied, principals worked deliberately to cultivate belief in everyone's capacity to improve and succeed.

Lezotte and Snyder (2011) concluded that high expectations for success included two critical beliefs. School personnel had to believe that students possessed the ability to succeed. Also, the school personnel had to believe that they had the capacity to enable all students to achieve success. We found considerable evidence of these two beliefs in all of the high-performing urban schools we studied.

Cultivating belief, when students, parents, and school personnel have experienced years of failure, can be very challenging. Students may perceive abundant evidence in their prior school performance, their test scores, or their friends' frustrations that success is unlikely. Parents who live in low-income situations might point to their own shattered educational dreams as proof that belief in their children's success is unwarranted. Teachers who experienced years of frustration trying to make a positive difference may have surrendered to feelings of helplessness as they considered the multiple, complex needs of their students.

Muhammad and Hollie (2012) explained that school personnel might hold beliefs that are counterproductive to the school's ability to generate excellent and equitable results. They contended:

> This is damaging when staff members hold beliefs and values that are different than those required for success in the school, such as when they discriminate against students based on race, social class, or disability. (p. 66)

In order to develop high-performing urban schools, the leaders we studied had to cultivate and sustain a high level of belief that educational success for all was possible. They did so by 1) modeling belief, 2) finding and celebrating evidence for belief, and 3) confronting disbelief.

Modeling Belief that All Students Will Improve and Succeed

We have never encountered a high-performing urban school in which key leaders were shocked to find that their students could achieve at high levels or stunned to realize that their team of educators had the capacity to teach well. Leaders believed, often before others believed.

In short, leaders inhaled the realities and challenges faced by their students, the students' families, and the school personnel; and then they exhaled belief, hope, and possibility hundreds of times, and in hundreds of ways, each day.

Leaders will not convince others to believe that success is possible if the leaders themselves do not believe. We have never encountered a high-performing urban school in which key leaders were shocked to find that their students could achieve at high levels or stunned to realize that their team of educators had the capacity to teach well. Leaders believed, often before others believed.

Teachers at C.E. Rose Elementary in Tucson, Arizona explained how, when only one-third of their students achieved proficiency in reading and mathematics, they acquired a new principal who was convinced that the school's predominantly low-income, Latino students could excel academically. At Boone Elementary in Kansas City, Missouri's Center School District, then-principal Sheryl Cochran assertively espoused the belief that their students (most of whom were Black and met low-income criteria) could perform at the advanced level (not just the basic or proficient level) on the state's new, very challenging assessment. "Good enough is not good enough," she said often, to express her conviction that Boone's students could achieve at the highest levels.

Gonzalez (2015) conducted an intensive study of an NCUST award-winning high school. In explaining the principal's impact on the school, Gonzalez stated:

The Arturo High [pseudonym] principal influenced many important changes as she articulated her expectations. In order to be to be able to articulate such consistently high expectations, the principal had to believe that academic success was possible for her students, including her Latino male students. Schools and districts must identify leaders who believe that all students deserve to have access to the best education. (p. 114)

By clearly and confidently expressing their high levels of belief, leaders compel others to re-examine their low levels of belief. Goddard, Hoy, and Hoy (2000) found that increases in teachers' belief in the capacity of their students to achieve and a staff's collective belief in their ability to teach students positively correlated with improvement in learning results. The researchers found that the staff's collective efficacy had a greater correlation with student achievement than did socio-economic variables. When leaders influence everyone's belief that their students can excel and the school faculty can succeed, leaders build collective efficacy. They increase the likelihood that everyone associated with the school will perceive that success is possible.

In the high-performing schools we studied, we consistently found principals and other school leaders who continuously espoused their belief that all of their students (and all demographic groups of students) would learn and succeed academically. In elementary, middle, and high schools, leaders openly shared their belief that the students served at their school could achieve impressive academic results and the school could become the kind of organization stakeholders desired. In faculty meetings, leaders at William Dandy Middle School in Fort Lauderdale, Florida regularly articulated their belief in the ability of their predominantly Black students to exceed (not just meet) state standards. Leaders at MacArthur Senior High School in Houston's Aldine Independent School District frequently attended teacher collaboration meetings during which they reinforced their conviction that educators could lead the school's students to college readiness. Parents at Sacramento's Golden Empire Elementary reported that the principal spoke passionately in parent-teacher organization meetings and in individual parent meetings about the capacity of all of the school's diverse populations of students to succeed. Teachers at Montebello Gardens Elementary in Los Angeles' Montebello Unified School District explained that their principal underscored her belief in the school's English learners to excel each time she visited classrooms and provided feedback. Leaders trumpeted their belief in students and school personnel through posters, murals, and signs at schools like Revere High School in Boston's Revere Public Schools, Horace Mann Elementary in the Glendale Unified School District in California, and dozens of other high-performing urban schools.

Even as principals addressed student behavior issues, attended special education placement meetings, worked with school personnel on master schedules, talked to students during passing periods, helped teachers problem-solve related to disagreements, met with individual parents, planned the use of Title I funds, addressed community business leaders, reported the achievement of different racial/ethnic groups of students, wrote items for weekly bulletins, organized recognition assemblies, or designed behavior improvement plans, they emphasized that the students served at the school could achieve at high levels, and they emphasized that their team of school personnel had the capacity to ensure all students would realize their learning potential. Terosky (2013) called this relentless pursuit of equity and excellence a "learning imperative"; that is " an obligation to prioritize, attend to, and act on matters of learning" above all else (p. 16).

Leaders in the high-performing urban schools were not blind to the challenges faced by their students, their neighborhoods, their school personnel, or their school districts. In fact, they knew these challenges in greater detail than almost anyone. Nonetheless, leaders chose to believe. Often, in our public speaking, we emphasize that the leaders of the high-performing schools we studied are not superheroes. They are mortals who faced typical urban school challenges with atypical levels of belief in the likelihood of success, even when evidence to support such belief was in short supply.

In short, leaders inhaled the realities and challenges faced by their students, the students' families, and the school personnel; and then they exhaled belief, hope, and possibility hundreds of times, and in hundreds of ways, each day. Some leaders were quiet and calm in the ways they expressed their belief in students, families, and school personnel. Some leaders were more passionate and expressive. Certainly, not all the leaders observed could be labeled charismatic; however, they all influenced the collective efficacy of their school.

Finding and Celebrating Evidence that Cultivates Belief

Before the schools we studied achieved impressive school-wide successes, leaders at these schools did an impressive job of finding, highlighting, and celebrating evidence that suggested success was attainable. Leaders identified and highlighted exemplary student work; mined data to find, expose, and celebrate evidence of progress and promise; and exposed school personnel to the progress and accomplishments of other high-performing urban schools that faced similar challenges.

Muhammad (2009) emphasized the importance of celebration in the culture of schools. He explained:

> Celebration in school provides consistent reinforcement about what is important. People often celebrate what they value, such as holidays and birthdays, for example. How schools celebrate learning and those who help students says a lot about how much the school values learning. (p. 105)

Leaders Promoted the Display of High-Quality Student Work

In our visits to high-performing urban schools, we found far more recent, high-quality student work posted and displayed than we find in typical urban schools. For example, at Maplewood Richmond Heights High School in St. Louis, all teachers posted exemplary student assignments. Typically, the rubric used to evaluate the assignment was also posted. The displayed student work provided indisputable evidence of the capacity of the school's students to achieve, while simultaneously motivating other students to produce work that similarly met the criteria specified in the rubric.

The use of classroom and hallway bulletin boards to highlight student work was common across high-performing urban schools. Often, principals encouraged teachers to highlight student writing. At Branch Brook Elementary in Newark, New Jersey, teachers posted writing that earned a "5" on the grade level's writing rubric. At Jim Thorpe Fundamental Academy in Santa Ana, California, hallways were lined with writing related to learning objectives in science, social studies, art, and other disciplines. At Dr. Charles T. Lunsford School in Rochester, New York, bulletin boards displayed students' friendly letters in which they explained to a classmate how to solve real-world, multiple-step mathematics problems. At James Pace Early College High School in Brownsville, Texas, the Spanish teacher posted detailed student reports, written in Spanish, highlighting the geography and culture of different Latin American countries.

Posted and displayed evidence of student accomplishment was prominent across multiple disciplines throughout the high-performing urban schools studied. In several of the schools, we saw student-developed science fair posters that reflected detailed inquiries into scientific phenomena. We saw trophies, plaques, and certificates earned by students for their success in robotics, dance, history, music, public speaking, spelling, mathematics, and other curricular and extra-curricular areas. Bulletin boards and display cases, filled with evidence of student accomplishment, stood as powerful rebuttals to anyone's disbelief about the capacity of the school's students to excel. At Revere High School in Boston, Massachusetts, a genius bar staffed by the school's students was a living display of the technological expertise students had developed.

Beyond the physical boundaries of the school, leaders displayed exemplary student work by engaging students in and with the community. For example, students at Dayton's Business Technology High School presented their detailed start-up business plans to members of the business community. At Maplewood Richmond Heights High School, students engaged in internships and community service activities that helped parents, community members, and business leaders appreciate the ability and the potential of the school's students. By positively influencing the beliefs of community members, leaders further advanced the collective efficacy of students and school personnel.

Leaders Found and Highlighted Evidence of Success in Data

Leaders created an atmosphere in which students, parents, and teachers felt that success was ubiquitous. Stakeholders and students felt that success was inevitable, in large part, because leaders celebrated progress as success.

In addition to highlighting the excellent work of individual students, leaders, working in collaboration with teachers, mined and exposed data that provided evidence of their students' capacity to excel and their teachers' ability to facilitate student success. In particular, leaders identified and celebrated successes reflected in common formative assessment data and in other short-cycle assessments of recently taught content. By focusing on results from short-duration, frequently administered assessments of recently taught content, leaders provided students and teachers evidence that success was attainable. For example, students at William Dandy Middle School could reasonably believe that, with appropriate effort, they could correctly answer the 10 math problems that focused exclusively on the objectives they had learned during the week. Teachers at Mallard Creek High School in Charlotte, North Carolina came to believe that they could create lessons that would lead all of their students to master the specific objectives that were central to each common formative assessment.

In contrast, leaders in more typical urban schools might spend much more time directing teachers' and students' attention to data from large-scale assessments that cover many objectives. Significant time may have elapsed since many of the assessed objectives were taught, leaving teachers and students feeling as though the opportunity to increase understanding and master content and skills had long since passed. While attention to such data has a place, it is less likely to lead teachers and students to believe that there are things they can do today (or at least this week) to ensure success.

In addition to focusing attention on short-cycle data, leaders in high-performing urban schools helped educators examine data in ways that illuminated potential for excellence. For example, in a typical urban school, leaders might bemoan formative assessment data that demonstrated only 20 percent of students with disabilities mastered the concept that teachers endeavored to teach. Alternately, we observed leaders in high-performing urban schools who greeted such data enthusiastically, asking teachers, "Who are the students with disabilities who mastered this tough objective? What did you do to help them achieve mastery? What strategies were most helpful? What could be done to extend those strategies to other students so that you might increase to 30 percent mastery or beyond?"

Datnow and Park (2014) emphasized that leaders should use data in a manner that supports "a culture of inquiry and continuous improvement" (p. 117). Also, they emphasized that leaders must "build trust in the process of data use" (p. 120). In the high-performing urban schools we studied, leaders promoted a culture of continuous improvement and inspired trust by making sincere efforts to identify evidence of growth and inspiring educators to learn from both small and large successes.

Continuously, leaders found and highlighted positive news in student data. Frequently, leaders pointed out the growth that students and teachers achieved. For example, at Eastwood Middle School, in El Paso, Texas, a math teacher explained that administrators at her school "always found the silver lining in our data." She elaborated:

> Whenever we look at the data and start to feel depressed because the results aren't as good as what we expected, an administrator will say, "it is pretty amazing how far you brought these students along in just a couple of weeks" or they'll say, "you got all of your students to master this part, so now you're most of the way to getting them to master the standard."

At Magnet Traditional School in Phoenix, as in many high-performing urban schools, the principal celebrated the progress of individual students, as well as the progress of entire classes and grade levels. Leaders created an atmosphere in which students, parents, and teachers felt that success was ubiquitous. Stakeholders and students felt that success was inevitable, in large part, because leaders celebrated *progress* as success. In an interview with students from Dayton Business Technology High School in Ohio a student explained:

> At my other school, you had to achieve honors in order to get anybody to know you existed. What were the chances of me getting honors? Zero! It was like the only way to get them to respect you was to hit a home run. Here, at this school, you just have to get to first base and they cheer you on. So, then you do all you can to get to second, and they cheer even more. Then third base, and then home, and then before you know it, you've accomplished the same as a home run. Here, they just make you feel like you can work hard and accomplish whatever you want in life.

Leaders Highlighted Evidence of Success in Similar Schools Serving Similar Students

In some of the high-performing urban schools we studied, we learned that leaders highlighted successes in similar schools in order to help school personnel believe that they could achieve better results. In some cases, leaders engaged groups of teachers and other school personnel in visits to schools that achieved impressive academic results for similar demographic groups of students. After these visits, leaders helped school personnel debrief and consider the capacity of their school to achieve similar or greater results.

In other cases, leaders led their faculties in book studies that focused upon high-performing urban schools. In the book studies, leaders helped their faculties understand that high levels of success were attainable through deliberate attention to improving school culture, curricula, and instruction.

Confronting Disbelief

Many of the leaders we interviewed told us that when achievement at their schools was low, there was considerable evidence that school personnel did not believe that all students could achieve. In many cases, educators articulated their negative beliefs openly. Also, leaders found evidence of a lack of belief in students in the various policies and practices implemented in the school. Muhammad and Hollie (2012, p. 66) asserted, "Leaders must confront these elephants in the room because they will begin to influence policies, practices, and procedures." In the schools we studied, leaders openly confronted the "elephants in the room." In order to move toward excellent and equitable learning results, leaders had to confront disbelief.

Confronting Verbalized Disbelief

While many of the leaders interviewed claimed that the number of school personnel who believed deeply in the capacity of the school's students to excel had increased substantially in recent years, we have not yet found a principal of a high-performing urban school who was convinced that every staff member at his or her school believed that all of the school's students could achieve at high levels. "I'm still working on a few people," was a common response to our inquiry. Nonetheless, principals and other school leaders were able to shift a critical mass of school personnel from a position of disbelief to a position of strong belief in the ability of all students to succeed academically and the capacity of school personnel to lead students to success. In many schools, leaders viewed their responses to publicly voiced disbelief as an essential component of their leadership practice.

Interviewees reported different styles and different levels of assertiveness in their leaders' responses when individuals suggested that students, or certain groups of students, could not achieve at high levels. For example, a teacher at R. N. Harris Elementary in Durham, North Carolina raised her eyebrows and asserted, "If someone suggested to our principal that these students could not succeed for any reason, she [the principal] would listen and then she would tell them clearly, plainly, and forcefully that she believed otherwise." In contrast, a teacher from William Dandy Middle School in Fort Lauderdale replied, "The past two principals would respond in slightly different ways. They would both be respectful. They would both make clear that they believed our kids could succeed. One was just more direct than the other."

Regardless of style, leaders rarely let negative comments go unchecked. "When someone says or does something to suggest that our students can't achieve," explained the teacher leader at Franklin Elementary in Bakersfield, California, "that has to be addressed. We have to talk about it and unpack it and help people see the truth." Similarly, the principal of Cecil H. Parker Elementary in Mount Vernon, New York explained:

> If you don't respond to negative comments like that, you let those ideas fester and grow. It's best to deal with it quickly and respectfully. You have to show that you believe in the students, but you also believe in the person who made the negative comment.

Leaders often framed their rebuttals to disbelief in ways that emphasized the moral underpinnings of their perspective. For instance, Newsome (2015) described his rebuttal to the negative beliefs he encountered as a superintendent in a district with rapidly increasing diversity by stating:

> I also talked to the group about my experience at the school board's public engagement session earlier in the school year, and my disappointment in hearing some students being referred to as "those kids." I explained that I was once one of "those kids." My brothers and sister and my parents were "those kids." Additionally, I pointed out the fact that some of the teachers in the audience were also "those kids" at some time in their lives. "Those kids" was the term used to describe students who did not conveniently fit into our comfort box . . . My focus was on the needs of every student and appealing to the core beliefs of our teachers who genuinely wanted to do their best to help students . . . During the seven years since this session, I have never heard anyone in our district use the term "those kids" again . . . not once. (p. 242)

Often principals tried to respond constructively without embarrassing or humiliating the individual who expressed the negative comment. By doing so, leaders affirmed their belief in their students, but they also affirmed their belief in their colleagues.

Clearly, much of the disbelief that obstructs the pursuit of excellence and equity is connected to conceptualizations of race/ethnicity, language background, and socio-economic status. Often disbelief concerning the capacity of students of color to perform well academically lurks just below the surface of comments that act like red traffic lights, stopping movement toward the cultural, curricular, and/or instructional changes that might advance excellence and equity. In the high-performing schools we studied, leaders did not shy away from discussions about race, ethnicity, or language. Browne (2012) suggested that culturally courageous leaders are *consummate conciliators* who are willing to engage people in discussions about biases, stereotypes, or negative assumptions in ways that help groups address difficult issues and move forward toward practices that will promote excellence and equity. As well, Browne argued that culturally courageous leaders are *committed caregivers* who are willing to stand up and speak out on behalf of all students and all student groups.

Confronting Disbelief in Policies and Practices

At times, leaders chose to confront disbelief through specific policies and practices. For example, at Lawndale High School in Los Angeles, an administrator explained that the school's former grading policy was set up "to affirm that some students were destined to not learn." The administrator explained:

> We had so many students passing courses with D grades. Sometimes, they got a D mostly because they showed up. They didn't really learn anything. They had not learned enough to succeed at the next level. We made it OK for kids to not learn and we told ourselves it was OK because you "couldn't really expect more from these kids." Well, we had to change that. We [the faculty] talked about it and we realized that none of us really liked the way things were going, but we had been acting like we had no choice. Then, we

figured that we did have a choice. We didn't have to allow anyone to get a D grade. So, at our school, we instituted a "No D" policy. In order to pass, you have to earn a C. We give kids lots of chances. We support them. We do everything we can to help them earn at least a C. But, we don't let them just get by and not learn anything.

In many of the high-performing schools, we found similar situations in which leaders challenged policies and practices that seemed to suggest that some students would not or could not succeed. Furman (2012) observed that such social justice-oriented leadership is "action oriented" and "involves identifying and undoing . . . oppressive and unjust practices and replacing them with more equitable, culturally appropriate ones" (p. 194).

As mentioned in Chapter 1, in order to qualify for the National Excellence in Urban Education Award, schools had to have low suspension rates for every racial/ethnic group they served. Davis and Jordan (1994) demonstrated how suspensions, and similar disciplinary actions that removed students from instruction, were negatively associated with student achievement. By requiring evidence of low suspension rates for every racial/ethnic served, NCUST sought affirmation that all students received the opportunity to learn, graduate, and excel. At many of the award-winning schools, suspensions occurred only when mandated by state or district policy. For example, suspensions were rare at Maplewood Richmond Heights High School in St. Louis. However, when the principal first arrived at the school, behavior incidents and out-of-school suspensions occurred frequently. The principal recognized that out-of-school suspensions were not reducing disciplinary incidents. Instead, suspensions reinforced a punitive culture that separated students who were able to manage their behavior from those who seemed unable to do so. Similarly, at Edison Public School Academy in Detroit, Michigan, when the principal first began his assignment at the school, teachers were suspending kindergarten students in great numbers. Immediately, the principal said, "No more."

Working with the teachers and other school personnel, these two principals challenged the effectiveness of old discipline policies and led the schools to institute restorative practices that improved the schools' climate, provided students opportunities to support one another in behaving appropriately, reduced disciplinary incidents, and helped all students feel valued and respected.

School leaders challenged policies and practices related to homework, grading, absences, school supplies, grouping/tracking, access to advanced classes, and many other day-to-day concerns. When policies and practices seemed counter-productive to the goal of ensuring the success of all students, leaders helped school personnel recognize that they could institute more effective ways of working with students. Typically, leaders did not dictate solutions, but instead they supported school personnel as they considered research and best practices that could lead to better learning outcomes for all groups of students.

Summary

To move their urban schools toward high performance for all demographic groups, leaders influenced the extent to which stakeholders 1) believed that all students had the ability to succeed at high levels, and 2) believed that school personnel had the capacity to ensure the success of their students. While this task is rarely easy and never complete, it is impossible if the leader does not model a compelling belief through both words and deeds. With great consistency and persistence, leaders modeled their belief in the school's students and the school's personnel. While leaders acknowledged the many challenges that confronted improvement efforts, they stood firm in their belief that all demographic groups of students could excel, they inspired hope, and they made it easier for others to believe that equity and excellence were attainable.

To reinforce the perception that success was within reach, leaders engaged school personnel (and sometimes students and parents) in identifying and showcasing examples of success. In many high-performing urban schools, a snowballing effect was triggered as the celebration of learning and achievement inspired increased effort that led to more accomplishment and more celebration of learning and achievement and so on. Bulletin boards, display cases, and hallway walls exhibited concrete evidence that the school's students could learn and the school's personnel could teach. Similarly, leaders engaged others in examining data for the specific purpose of finding and highlighting evidence of success. In such an environment, it is easy to see how a critical mass of students, parents, and school personnel would come to believe, and even expect, that all students would achieve at high levels.

Still, it is important to note that leaders confronted many obstacles as they sought to influence beliefs about student ability. In many cases, disbelief was clearly associated with race/ethnicity, language background, and/or socio-economic status. Leaders found ways to confront the disbelief they encountered openly, yet respectfully. Leaders found ways to communicate their strong belief in the ability of students, while simultaneously expressing their strong belief in the capacity of their school personnel. In confronting disbelief, leaders were also wise enough to recognize that disbelief was often embedded within policies and practices that made it difficult or impossible for success to occur. In these cases, leaders listened carefully and encouraged both creativity and courage as stakeholders considered better options for serving students.

What It Is & What It Isn't: Leadership that Influences Belief in the Capacity to Improve

What It Is: Modeling Belief that All Students Will Succeed Academically

It is plain to students, parents, and school personnel that school leaders are convinced that all groups of students served by the school are likely to succeed educationally. All of the leaders' words and actions convey a certainty about the ability of students to succeed and the capacity of school personnel to ensure student success.

What It Isn't: Sending Inconsistent Messages about Beliefs

School leaders rarely share their beliefs about the ability of students to succeed. When leaders articulate their beliefs, some stakeholders assume that leaders are making politically correct statements, because they rarely see evidence to suggest that leaders actually believe that all students at the school can achieve at high levels.

* * *

What It Is: Finding and Celebrating Evidence that Cultivates Belief

Leaders shape the physical environment in ways that promote the regular cele-bration of high-quality student work. In particular, leaders encourage the identifica-tion and display of recent, exemplary student work in hallways, on bulletin boards, in classrooms, and in display cases. Evidence of student ability to excel is made obvious in all corners of the school. Almost every student can find some acknow-ledgment of his or her good work displayed somewhere in the school.

What It Isn't: Using Space in a Way that Affirms Negative Beliefs about Student Ability

Classrooms, hallways, and bulletin boards include few examples of recent student work. The work displayed often reflects relatively low expectations, and displays of work are often months old before they are replaced. The only students whose efforts are celebrated in displays of work are the students considered the most academically talented.

* * *

What It Is: Finding and Celebrating Evidence that Cultivates Belief

Leaders constantly work with school personnel to review data and find evidence of success and accomplishment. Yes, leaders engage school personnel in looking for opportunities for improvement, but substantial attention is focused on identifying progress and understanding the reasons why progress occurred. Leaders celebrate progress in ways that make others believe that additional progress and success are likely. Leaders continuously celebrate the accomplishments of individual students, classrooms, grade levels, departments, and the entire school.

What It Isn't: Focusing on Data Only to Find Evidence of Failure

Leaders engage stakeholders in examining data; however, the purpose is almost exclusively to find evidence of shortcoming and failure. The typical focus is on ques-tions such as, "What percentage of students did not meet the standard? How many students failed? What wasn't taught well? What needs to be improved?" Even when successes are identified, they aren't celebrated. Sometimes successes are used to humiliate teachers and/or students who fall short of success.

* * *

What It Is: Confronting Disbelief

Leaders persistently, yet respectfully, confronted individuals who expressed dis-belief about the ability of students to succeed. They do not seek to embarrass disbe-lievers; however, they do not allow negative assertions to control the school culture. Similarly, leaders carefully consider policies and practices that might reinforce dis-belief. Leaders encourage stakeholders to think creatively about alternatives that better convey a belief that all students can succeed.

What It Isn't: Allowing Disbelief to Fester and Grow

Leaders ignore statements that suggest that the school's students (or certain groups of the school's students) cannot or will not succeed. By doing so, leaders imply their agreement. In some cases, they allow others to highjack the leadership roles that ultimately shape the school's culture. Similarly, leaders ignore the policies or practices that reinforce disbelief. Leaders act as if those policies or practices cannot or should not be changed, so they persist, along with the negative beliefs they reinforce.

School Self-Assessment Tool: Does Your School Leadership Positively Influence Belief in the Capacity to Improve and Succeed?

This self-assessment will help you determine the extent to which leadership at your school influences stakeholders' beliefs about students' capacity to improve and success and about the school's capacity to ensure student success. Consider engaging teams of teachers, administrators, parents, and students to respond to these questions. (One could invite participants to provide individual ratings and then compile separate ratings for stakeholder groups.) Completion of the self-assessment will generate a picture of the school's current practices. By utilizing the same process annually or semi-annually, the school community can assess progress in influencing the desire to change. Rate the following on a scale of 1 to 5, with 1 representing NOT LIKELY and 5 representing VERY LIKELY.

I. How likely is it that students (including all demographic groups of students) perceive that school leaders believe that they are likely to succeed academically and in life? Rating _____

If different demographic groups of students would be likely to respond to this item differently, explain to what extent responses would vary and why: _____

II. How likely is it that school personnel perceive that their school leaders believe that they are likely to succeed in ensuring the academic success of all students at the school? Rating _____

If the answer to this item might differ regarding ensuring the success of different demographic groups of students, explain to what extent responses would vary and why: _____

III. To what extent do school leaders consistently convey a strong belief that all students served by the school can improve and succeed academically? Rating _____

If the answer to this item might differ when considering different demographic groups of students, explain to what extent responses would vary and why: _____

IV. To what extent do school leaders consistently convey a strong belief that all school personnel can ensure the academic success of all groups of students? Rating _____

If the answer to this item might differ when considering different demographic personnel groups, explain to what extent responses would vary and why: _____

V. To what extent does the school celebrate high-quality student work by posting it prominently and attractively, changing the examples posted regularly, and maintaining high standards for displayed work? Rating _____

VI. To what extent does the school celebrate high-quality student work through exhibitions, assemblies, community projects, and other efforts that bring attention to learning and accomplishment? Rating _____

VII. To what extent do school leaders consistently identify, highlight, and celebrate progress and growth in student data? Rating _____

VIII. When individuals articulate disbelief in the ability of the school's students to succeed, how likely is it that leaders will respond in an assertive yet respectful manner? Rating _____

IX. To what extent do school leaders cause stakeholders to question policies and practices that reinforce disbelief in the ability of students to succeed? How likely are leaders to encourage and support the adoption of new policies and practices that might reinforce positive beliefs about student ability? Rating _____

References

Browne II, J.R. (2012). *Walking the equity talk: A guide for culturally courageous leadership in school communities.* Thousand Oaks, CA: Corwin.

Datnow, A., & Park, V. (2014). *Data-driven leadership.* San Francisco, CA: Jossey-Bass.

Davis, J.E., & Jordan, W.J. (1994). The effects of school context, structure, and experiences on African American males in middle and high school. *Journal of Negro Education, 63*(4), 570–587.

Furman, G. (2012). Social justice leadership as praxis: Developing capacities through preparation programs. *Educational Administration Quarterly, 48,* 191–229.

Goddard, R.D., Hoy, W.K., & Hoy, A.W. (2000). Collective teacher efficacy: Its meaning, measure, and effect on student achievement. *American Education Research Journal, 37*(2), 479–507.

Gonzalez, M. (2015). *Latino males and academic achievement* (Order No. 3687899). Available from ProQuest Dissertations & Theses A&I; ProQuest Dissertations & Theses Full Text: The Humanities and Social Sciences Collection (1669909945).

Lezotte, L.W., & Snyder, K.M. (2011). *What effective schools do: Re-envisioning the correlates.* Bloomington, IN: Solution Tree Press.

Muhammad, A. (2009). *Transforming school culture: How to overcome staff division.* Bloomington, IN: Solution Tree Press.

Muhammad, A., & Hollie, S. (2012). *The will to lead, the skill to teach: Transforming schools at every level.* Bloomington, IN: Solution Tree Press.

Newsome, M.J. (2015). A journey toward equity and excellence for all students in Chesterfield. In A.M. Blankstein & P. Noguera (eds.), *Excellence through equity: Five principles of courageous leadership to guide achievement for every student* (pp. 239–258). Thousand Oaks, CA: Corwin.

Terosky, A.L. (2013). From a managerial imperative to a learning imperative: Experiences of urban public school principals, *Educational Administration Quarterly, 50*(1), 3–33. DOI: 10.1177/0013161X13488597.

Leadership that Influences Clarity about Roles and Responsibilities

7

The educator Horace Mann wrote,"Let us not be content to wait and see what will happen, but give us the determination to make the right things happen." How do we make the right things happen? How do we structure our school so that these right things are always kept alive? When I started at Horace Mann, we were the lowest school in the district. We were really struggling. We made a lot of excuses often based on the lack of resources or limited background experiences many of our English learners and high-poverty students brought to school. My job was to help us figure out what we were going to do about it. So, we started looking at data. We clearly saw that reading comprehension was our lowest area. Vocabulary and writing were also areas of need. The large achievement gaps between our sub-groups, especially between our Hispanic students and the overall district performance, were big concerns. In the classroom, there was a lot of inconsistency in instructional practices and curriculum. Lesson delivery was erratic. Rigor varied from teacher to teacher, even within the same grade level. We seemed to be working more as independent contractors than as grade-level or school teams.

Based on the needs of our students, what were the right things that we wanted to prioritize and make happen? We knew we had to concentrate our efforts in order to get results. So, we started by making sure that we all had a clear instructional focus. Our instructional focus was improving reading comprehension. Therefore, we initially focused on learning the reading comprehension standards: What are they asking students to do? What does proficiency look like at our grade level? What are the highest priority standards? How are we going to teach them? We wanted to make sure teachers had a common understanding of what students were expected to do and understand. We had to work together in order to steadily improve student achievement each year. By identifying the most critical standards, we were able to spend time carefully analyzing the standards, planning strong lessons as grade levels, and developing common assessments to measure students' progress in mastering those standards. We also identified research-based practices to support our teaching of the reading comprehension standards, including Reciprocal Teaching, QAR (Question–Answer Relationship), and student engagement.

We implemented structures to facilitate our work to improve the teaching and learning of the comprehension standards. For example, we extended our school day so that we banked minutes and then, one day a week, we had a shorter school day. During the shortened day, we have meeting times. Teachers meet in grade-level teams so they have collaboration time to design lessons based on the focus standards, and identify lesson objectives. They're asking, "How do we break down the thinking process so students understand and can perform at a rigorous standard?"

They call these thinking processes "How-to-do-it Steps." During these collaboration meetings, they also have time to look at student work to analyze students' performance on the grade-level developed assessment. They discuss what does proficient performance look like? What were areas of difficulty and what are next steps to improve students' understanding? They identify which students got it and which students didn't, but more importantly, they feel empowered to make the right things happen to improve student achievement, starting one step at a time.

Rosa Alonso, Principal, Horace Mann
Elementary School, Glendale, CA

Leaders in high-performing urban schools, like the principal at Horace Mann Elementary, helped stakeholders understand their specific roles and responsibilities in establishing a positive transformational culture, challenging curricula, and engaging, effective instruction. Not only did leaders build the desire to improve and the belief that improvement was possible, they also developed shared understandings of the essential work to be done in order to realize improvements.

Generating clarity about the most critical aspects of roles and responsibilities takes careful thought and precise communication. Popular professional development programs offer dozens of prescriptions as educators seek to improve learning results (e.g., differentiated instruction, data-based decision making, professional learning communities, English language development, project-based learning, integrated instruction, small-group instruction, personalized instruction, gradual release of responsibility, higher-order questioning strategies). Often school personnel are overwhelmed with the multitude of programs and approaches they are asked to integrate into their daily work. As well, clarity is often evasive, as inconsistent definitions, images, or representations of quality implementation are commonplace in schools. For example, three teachers might all believe that they implement Program Z well; however, they might all have different understandings of Program Z, its components, implementation criteria, and rationale. Each teacher might have different understandings of what can and cannot be modified, adapted, omitted, or supplemented. They might have very different understandings of what might represent quality implementation, and they might not have any understanding of how quality implementation might be measured. Yet, all three teachers attended the Program Z workshops. They all have the Program Z Certificate on their classroom walls. And, they all consider themselves knowledgeable, if not expert, about Program Z. Consequently, the naive leader who enters the school, suggesting that Program Z be implemented, is likely to encounter a "been there and done that" response, even if teachers are implementing Program Z poorly or inconsistently.

In the absence of clarity and consistency about the factors that will influence development of culture, curricula, and instruction in ways that lead to excellent and equitable learning results, schools are not likely to make sustainable progress. Even as leaders convince stakeholders that their efforts are worthwhile and that success is attainable, leaders must also help stakeholders understand what they must do in order to support student success. Roles and expectations must be clearly communicated and consistently understood.

Generating clarity about the most critical aspects of roles and responsibilities takes careful thought and precise communication. Popular professional development programs offer dozens of prescriptions as educators seek to improve learning results (e.g., differentiated instruction, data-based decision making, professional learning communities, English language development, project-based learning, integrated instruction, small-group instruction, personalized instruction, gradual release of responsibility, higher-order questioning strategies, etc.). Often school personnel are overwhelmed with the multitude of programs and approaches they are asked to integrate into their daily work. As well, clarity is often evasive, as inconsistent definitions, images, or representations of quality implementation are commonplace in schools. For example, three teachers might all believe that they implement Program Z well; however, they might all have different understandings of Program Z, its components, implementation criteria, and rationale. Each teacher might have different understandings of what can and cannot be modified, adapted, omitted, or supplemented. They might have very different understandings of what might represent quality implementation, and they might not have any understanding of how quality implementation might be measured. Yet, all three teachers attended the Program Z workshops. They all have the Program Z Certificate on their classroom walls. And, they all consider themselves knowledgeable, if not expert, about Program Z. Consequently, the naive leader who enters the school, suggesting that Program Z be implemented, is likely to encounter a "been there and done that" response, even if teachers are implementing Program Z poorly or inconsistently.

In the absence of clarity and consistency about the factors that will influence the development of culture, curricula, and instruction in ways that lead to excellent and equitable learning results, schools are not likely to make sustainable progress. Even as leaders convince stakeholders that their efforts are worthwhile and that success is attainable, leaders must also help stakeholders understand what they must do in order to support student success. Roles and expectations must be clearly communicated and consistently understood.

Clear, Consistent, and Regular Communication of Expectations

Stakeholders knew what their leaders expected, not by what the leader announced in staff meetings or assemblies, but by what the leader observed, commented upon, and/or celebrated each and every day.

To create a coherent educational improvement system, leaders in high-performing urban schools made sure that all members of the system understood the interdependent nature of the roles they assumed. Leaders communicated clearly, consistently, and regularly with students, parents, teachers, support personnel, and other stakeholders in ways that helped them understand how they, as individuals, each contributed to a school-wide effort to generate excellent and equitable learning results.

It is important to understand that leaders typically addressed the challenge of communicating roles and expectations in ways that simultaneously addressed the aforementioned leadership challenge of influencing stakeholders' desire to change and improve (see Chapter 5). This means that, in the high-performing schools we studied, leaders did not act in a dictatorial manner, listing edicts and demanding compliance. Instead, we observed leaders helping stakeholders understand why certain roles, responsibilities, and expectations could make a profound difference in the lives of the students served. Leaders nurtured the collective will to assume critical roles. One example can be found in the statement made by a teacher at William Dandy Middle School in Fort Lauderdale. In describing why the school modified the master schedule to create Success Days in response to common formative assessment data, the teacher explained:

> The principal kept us talking about how we could get more students to show that they had really learned the concepts we were trying to teach in each unit. She kept pointing to the data and asking us how some teachers managed to get almost all of their students to master the content. The idea of Success Days came out of those discussions. We kind of threw out the master schedule for a few days while we learned from the successes of some of the teachers who were really getting students to mastery. The ones [teachers] with the best results taught the students and kind of taught the rest of us at the same time. I'm not sure who came up with the idea. I guess it was all of us.

In the schools we studied, leaders nurtured shared commitments related to specific roles and responsibilities. For example, the principal at Harris Elementary in Georgia's Gwinnett County Public Schools encouraged teachers to commit to delivering high-quality differentiated instruction. The principal at Feaster Charter School in Chula Vista, California was able to lead teachers to commit to utilizing weekly, two-hour, grade-level meetings to maximize teacher collaboration in ways that improved lesson quality and effectiveness. At Maplewood Richmond Heights High School in St. Louis, a school where students had traditionally experienced difficulty completing a day without fistfights, the principal led students to commit to a set of principles and processes related to restorative justice. Typically leaders in these and many other high-performing urban schools communicated and reinforced their expectations by noticing when stakeholders fulfilled expectations or made progress toward fulfilling expectations.

Stakeholders knew what their leaders expected, not by what the leader announced in staff meetings or assemblies, but by what the leader observed, commented upon, and/or celebrated each and every day. Throughout the high-performing schools studied, leaders spent major portions of each school day or each school week in classrooms. The time leaders spent in classrooms was utilized to notice, highlight, and acknowledge teachers' efforts to assume critical roles and responsibilities.

In response to the question, "How do you know what your principal truly expects from you when you're teaching?" a teacher at Jim Thorpe Fundamental Academy in Santa Ana, California invited the interviewer to "come and see this." The teacher opened a drawer that was filled with small notes left by the principal during her walk-through visits. Then, the teacher continued to explain:

> She always does this. And the notes are usually about the same things like rigor and engagement. Most of the notes are very kind and positive, but they are focused on what I did to keep the kids engaged or what I did to get them to think or how I challenged them. This is what she pays attention to. So we deliver. We get really good at teaching the way she wants us to teach.

Often teachers commented that their leaders were clear and direct in providing feedback. Typically, teachers reported that they appreciated the direct approach, because it was usually positive and always constructive. Codrington (2015) reported in her study of an NCUST award-winning school that teachers appreciated the principal's frequent classroom observations. One teacher explained:

> She [the principal] is very straightforward. You know and you understand her expectations, and she makes no bones about it. Everybody's on board. I think people respect that. When you come shooting straight and telling people what you expect, [as well as] the purpose behind it, people can accept that. (p. 119)

Teachers and other stakeholders acknowledged that their leaders had high expectations. Many teachers reported that they worked harder than they had been required to work at other schools. At the same time, they reported they were willing to work hard, because the clearly communicated expectations were helping them to generate better learning results for all students.

In communicating expectations, leaders often made clear how their expectations were intended to influence the various groups of students served in the school. For example, at Montebello Gardens Elementary in Los Angeles, the principal emphasized the expectation of engaging students in discourse about every topic presented. While this was a general expectation, teachers reported that the principal was particularly passionate about ensuring that English learners were both pushed and supported so that they would constantly be engaged in discourse about important concepts.

In a similar manner, students reported that their school leaders had clear and unambiguous expectations for their work and their behavior. "You can't just come here to cruise like you did in the other high school," explained a student at Dayton Business Technology High School. The student continued, "People expect you to constantly use your mind, ask questions, and try to apply what you're being taught."

A student at Maplewood Richmond Heights High School in St. Louis offered a similar explanation of his principal's expectations.

> He [the principal] expects you to go to college. So, he really expects you to act like you're going to college or like you're already there. Whether we're in a class or at an event or just walking in between classes, we know what he expects: college behavior. If you don't behave that way, you can be sure he's going to say something. If you do behave that way, you can be sure he's going to notice.

Prioritizing and De-Prioritizing Roles and Responsibilities

Leaders helped stakeholders develop clear understandings of critical roles and responsibilities by prioritizing what was most important and de-prioritizing other tasks. Typically, leaders emphasized only a few priorities related to student behavior and engagement. Similarly, leaders emphasized only a few priorities regarding everyday classroom instruction. Johnson, Uline, and Perez (2011) found that leaders of high-performing urban schools tended to focus attention on only a few key elements of instructional effectiveness during classroom observations. In particular, principals focused upon evidence of student engagement, student learning, and/or student understanding. They also emphasized classroom climate, tone, or atmosphere. By addressing these issues consistently, leaders helped ensure that everyone understood these issues were of primary importance. At the same time, however, leaders de-emphasized many other matters that had little relationship with the main areas of focus.

Some leaders may have difficulty promoting clarity about key roles and responsibilities because they lead school personnel to believe that there are innumerable priorities. In sharp contrast, a teacher at high-performing Wasena Elementary in Roanoke, Virginia explained:

> This is a great place to teach because the principal makes it a great place. We're not drowning in a thousand programs and initiatives and every-other-day changes, like happens at some schools. At this school, you know that there are a few things that are really important and you can focus on those and actually succeed. And, then you see the difference it makes to the students.

We have heard principals in struggling schools argue earnestly that there are so many critical needs that they cannot possibly reduce the number of priorities they need teachers and other personnel to address. Of course, a simple response is to note the lack of measurable progress made when the leader has insisted that educators focus on dozens of concerns all at once. Another response can be found in the words of a district administrator in Houston's Aldine Independent School District (the home of several NCUST award-winning schools). The administrator suggested:

> It's all about how you frame what is important. If you focus on small things, people will be frustrated, because they will need to address many small things and one missed small thing might make a big difference in whether or not all the other things you did have any impact. If, instead, you focus on big things, you can have just a few big items that combine to make a big difference. In this district, we say, "You've got to keep the main thing the main thing." Principals can't make everything the main thing, or they'll drive themselves and their people crazy.

The logic of pursuing a few major areas of focus prevailed among almost all leaders of the high-performing schools we studied. Even when leaders inherited highly dysfunctional school environments, they resisted the temptation to insist that educators fix every issue. Instead, they helped teachers perceive that progress was attainable by asking educators to focus on a limited set of concerns and corresponding strategies. As the principal of Jim Thorpe Fundamental Academy in Santa Ana explained, "After we got really good at one thing, we took on something else that seemed necessary. We didn't try to do it all at once."

Promoting Inquiry and Flexibility

While leaders promoted clarity about critical roles, responsibilities, and expectations, educators continued to feel empowered as thoughtful, creative professionals. In fact, leaders expected school personnel to pinpoint problems, think creatively, and generate solutions tailored to the unique situations presented by their students. Leaders balanced attention to specific strategies and approaches with the need to provide educators with a sense of autonomy and flexibility as they endeavored to ensure the academic success of all students.

In many of the high-performing urban schools, leaders framed expectations on *what* teachers should accomplish; yet they offered substantial flexibility regarding *how* teachers met expectations in ways that maximized student learning. For example, at Southside Elementary Museums Magnet School in Miami-Dade County, Florida, the principal expected all teachers to include a three-dimensional object as a focal point of each lesson. Teachers used collaboration opportunities to plan how they would meet this expectation in everyday lessons throughout the curriculum. Similarly, at World of Inquiry School in Rochester, New York, the focus on experiential learning was not negotiable. The principal expected to see abundant evidence of hands-on activities and projects that integrated learning objectives across disciplines. Simultaneously, however, the principal encouraged teachers to work together once a week during "Are we there yet?" meetings. In these meetings, teachers planned creatively, reviewed student work, analyzed data, designed new interdisciplinary projects, and monitored progress related to student learning goals. These routines promoted a spirit of inquiry among the teachers, just as the teachers endeavored to promote a spirit of inquiry among students.

In many of the high-performing urban schools studied, leaders expected teachers to build high levels of academic rigor into each lesson. In classroom observations, leaders looked for evidence that students were developing deep understandings of challenging concepts and skills. Leaders looked for evidence that students were able to apply what they were learning to real-life situations, synthesize information, reach conclusions, and make reasonable predictions. At the same time, leaders encouraged and expected teachers to work together to design the lessons that would promote rigor. For example, at MC^2 STEM High School in Cleveland, Ohio, the principal expected teachers to work together with community partners to create powerful experiences for students in science, technology, mathematics, and engineering. Similarly, the principal at Hillside University Demonstration School in the San Bernardino City Unified School District expected teachers to work together to plan how they would utilize iPads, project-based learning, and daily small-group enrichment activities to ensure that all students mastered rigorous learning objectives.

Frey and Fisher (2004) described the role of quality questions in promoting academic rigor. In several of the high-performing schools, leaders focused attention specifically on the questions teachers asked to influence the depth of students' thinking. For example, at Stehlik Intermediate School in Houston's Aldine Independent School District, a teacher explained:

> Our principal really pushes for rigor. We have to post rigorous objectives, we have to use flexible, small-group instruction, and we have to use a variety of questioning techniques to get students to think deeply enough to master

the objective. What makes this school a great place to work is that we [the teachers] get so much support on this from each other. In our team meetings, we're constantly helping each other think about our questioning strategies and giving each other ideas. It's fun to meet high expectations when you know clearly what is expected and when you know you can be creative in figuring out how to meet the expectations.

Many of the teachers we interviewed reported that they were invigorated by opportunities to use their backgrounds, experience, and knowledge to design powerful lessons that led all students to mastery. As a teacher at Eastwood Middle School in El Paso's Ysleta Independent School District explained:

This is a great place to teach, because I get to bring all that I know, all my experience, and all that I believe in service to my colleagues and our students. We expect a lot of ourselves here, but I like coming to work because we're constantly thinking, problem solving, and creating. We're constantly thinking about how we can make lessons work for our kids. And, we keep getting better.

Summary

In the high-performing urban schools studied, leaders built shared understandings of the essential work to be done in order to generate improvements. Leaders emphasized what teachers, other school personnel, students, and parents needed to do in order to contribute to school-wide efforts to ensure excellent and equitable learning results. Often, these shared understandings were initiated through the leader's knowledge and experience. When leaders possess a strong base of understanding about culture, curricula, and instruction, they are equipped to offer clear, powerful descriptions of the roles teachers (and other stakeholders) need to assume in order to bring about excellent and equitable learning results. It is important to note, however, that generally, leaders did not dictate expectations. They worked with stakeholders to reach a shared understanding of which roles, responsibilities, and expectations were appropriate, given their shared goals.

Leaders did far more than introduce their expectations related to roles and responsibilities. Leaders communicated and reinforced their expectations by noticing when and how stakeholders made progress toward expectations and by providing feedback, offering suggestions, and celebrating evidence of progress. Stakeholders knew that their leaders were constantly watching for evidence of progress on the concerns leaders perceived as most important.

To minimize confusion about what was most important, leaders made clear the few key roles and responsibilities they expected stakeholders to assume. At the same time, leaders reduced the emphasis on other matters and responsibilities. By prioritizing and de-prioritizing issues, leaders made it easier for stakeholders to focus on making essential improvements.

Finally, leaders helped stakeholders perceive that they had opportunities to exercise considerable latitude, flexibility, and creativity, even as leaders specified performance expectations. In fact, leaders helped stakeholders (especially school personnel) understand that part of their responsibility was to use their knowledge, background, and experience to address roles and responsibilities creatively. In particular, leaders expected collaboration opportunities to yield new and creative ways to solve educational challenges and better meet the needs of students.

What It Is & What It Isn't: Leadership that Influences Clarity about Roles and Responsibilities

What It Is: Emphasizing Roles that Lead to Better Culture, Curricula, and Instruction

School leaders emphasize roles, responsibilities, and expectations that have a clear relationship to establishing a positive transformational culture, challenging academic curricula, and engaging, effective instruction. People are not likely to wonder why the leader emphasizes specific roles and responsibilities, because the leader constantly affirms the connection to excellent and equitable learning results.

What It Isn't: Emphasizing Roles Based on Fads and Trends

When the leader introduces a new expectation, stakeholders wonder, "Where did she get that idea?" Regularly, leaders introduce new roles and expectations without clear rationale. The issues that seemed important a few months ago are quietly forgotten as new issues emerge. When the leader leaves school to attend a professional development event, people wonder what new thing they will be expected to implement when the leader returns.

*   *   *

What It Is: Promoting Ownership of Roles, Responsibilities, and Expectations

Leaders give stakeholders the opportunity to see the data, the research, and the best practices that influenced the leader's thinking about key roles and responsibilities. As well, leaders listen to the ideas and concerns that others raise. The conversations about the most important roles and responsibilities are grounded in a shared focus on generating excellent and equitable learning results. Often stakeholders find the leader's ideas reasonable and logical. Often stakeholders perceive the expectation as jointly agreed upon and jointly constructed.

What It Isn't: Dictating Roles, Responsibilities, and Expectations

Leaders announce what others will be expected to do and offer little opportunity for stakeholder input. Sometimes stakeholders do not understand why they are asked to assume certain responsibilities. They simply know what the leader expects. As a result, one commonly observes resistance or token efforts to comply.

*   *   *

What It Is: Reinforcing Expectations by Noticing

Leaders notice the efforts stakeholders make to assume roles and responsibilities. Leaders notice and comment upon progress (even small amounts of progress) in ways that make stakeholders feel good about their efforts. Continuously, leaders notice, comment upon, and celebrate the implementation of roles and responsibilities.

What It Isn't: Reinforcing Expectations Only by Reminding (or Not at All)

Leaders articulate expectations orally or in writing, usually to groups. If there is any subsequent attention to the expectation, it comes through a reminder to the group. The leader rarely, if ever, notices whether or not stakeholders implement expectations. Quickly, stakeholders realize that nobody cares enough to notice whether they implement the expectation or not. Soon, the only ones acting upon the expectation are the ones who were doing so before the leader asked them to do so.

* * *

What It Is: Prioritizing and De-Prioritizing Responsibilities

Leaders repeatedly reinforce the same few priorities. They resist the temptation to add new priorities until they are confident that almost everyone has mastered the original ones. To help emphasize priorities, they deliberately reduce attention to other matters. Stakeholders feel like they have a higher likelihood of success because they can focus their attention on only a few key concerns.

What It Isn't: Making Everything a Priority

Leaders have long lists of roles, responsibilities, and expectations for stakeholders. Priorities, deemed important one day, are overshadowed by different priorities that arise the following day. Stakeholders are frustrated and confused.

* * *

What It Is: Promoting Inquiry and Flexibility

Working with stakeholders, leaders establish and develop shared understanding of primary expectations. Leaders encourage (and even expect) stakeholders to pursue the implementation of these expectations in ways that utilize their expertise, creativity, and best thinking. Stakeholders are invigorated by opportunities to determine how they can work together to implement key responsibilities in a manner that make a positive difference for students.

What It Isn't: Issuing Highly Prescriptive Mandates

Not only do leaders issue mandates, but they also do so in a manner that leaves educators little or no room for flexibility or creativity. Stakeholders feel undervalued, because they are not encouraged or allowed to utilize their knowledge, expertise, or creativity to shape implementation in ways that are likely to make a difference for students.

School Self-Assessment Tool: Does Your School Leadership Influence Clarity about Roles and Responsibilities?

This self-assessment will help you determine the extent to which leadership at your school influences clarity about roles and responsibilities. Consider engaging teams of teachers, administrators, parents, and students to respond to these questions. (One could invite participants to provide individual ratings and then compile separate ratings for stakeholder groups.) Completion of the self-assessment will generate a picture of the school's current practices. By utilizing the same process annually or semi-annually, the school community can assess progress in influencing the desire to change. Rate the following on a scale of 1 to 5, with 1 representing NOT LIKELY and 5 representing VERY LIKELY.

I. How likely is it that students (including all demographic groups of students) have a clear understanding of the few main things they need to do in order to succeed in school? Rating _____

If different demographic groups of students would be likely to respond to this item differently, explain to what extent responses would vary and why: _____

II. How likely is it that parents (including all demographic groups of parents) have a clear understanding of the few main things they need to do in order to help their children succeed in school? Rating

_____

If different demographic groups of parents would be likely to respond to this item differently, explain to what extent responses would vary and why: _____

III. How likely is it that school personnel (including various groups of school personnel) have a clear understanding of the few main things they need to do in order to play their roles in ways that contribute to all students succeeding in school? Rating _____

If different groups of school personnel would be likely to respond to this item differently, explain to what extent responses would vary and why: _____

IV. How likely is it that school leaders notice and comment upon the extent to which students (including all demographic groups of students) successfully address the few main things they need to do in order to succeed in school? Rating _____

If the answer varies for different demographic groups of students, explain to what extent the response would vary and why: _____

_____

V. How likely is it that school leaders notice and comment upon the extent to which parents (including parents of all demographic groups of students) successfully address the few main things they need to do in order to help their children succeed in school? Rating

_____

If the answer varies for different demographic groups of parents, explain to what extent the response would vary and why: _____

_____

VI. How likely is it that school leaders notice and comment upon the extent to which school personnel (including various groups of school personnel) successfully address the few main things they need to do in order to help students succeed in school? Rating ____

If different groups of school personnel would be likely to respond to this item differently, explain to what extent responses would vary and why: _____

VII. How likely is it that school personnel perceive that they are given an important role or responsibility, and that they are also given the opportunity to work together to use their knowledge, expertise, and creativity to generate effective strategies for implementing the roles and responsibilities? Rating _____

If different groups of school personnel would be likely to respond to this item differently, explain to what extent responses would vary and why: _____

References

Codrington, S. (2015). *Leadership practices that result in high achievement of African American students in an elementary school setting* (Order No. 3719628). Available from ProQuest Dissertations & Theses A&I; ProQuest Dissertations & Theses Full Text: The Humanities and Social Sciences Collection (1713693758).

Frey, D., & Fisher, N. (2004). *Improving adolescent literacy: Content area strategies at work.* Upper Saddle River, NJ: Pearson Education, Inc.

Johnson, J. F., Uline, C. L., & Perez, L. G. (2011). Expert noticing and principals of high-performing urban schools. *Journal of Education for Students Placed at Risk, 16,* 122–136.

Leadership that Builds Capacity to Succeed

8

When I arrived at Finney, a model was in place to allow teachers time to get together during their day in grade levels for planning. As I observed the sessions, I noticed that they were planning just for one content area: writing. I was looking for evidence that the structure was grounded on the professional learning community practices, so by attending those meetings, I began building a relationship with my team. Initially, I did not observe in their plans a method to gauge whether or not students were meeting the intended outcomes. I encountered more of a calendaring of activities, driven by a desire to cover all of the content on the summative state test. The state's released test questions were driving the conversations. I wanted to see more of a relationship between the planning and impact in the classrooms. I recognized right away that this was just test prep. But, I knew that relationship building was important. I had to get to know my team and I had to begin the process of evolving my team without fracturing any of the relationships I needed. I knew we had to go deep and I knew I had to get them all on board. My challenge was always the relationship piece balanced with the pressure I felt because I knew that the kids couldn't wait. They needed help right away.

The teachers needed a better picture of what a PLC should be. So, we studied Marzano's work and we studied other models for PLCs. Once we better defined what a PLC should be and accomplish, we committed to extending the planning focus. So, over the years, we went from a writing focus, to a merged literacy block (it's an integrated close reading and writing segment). And, we also plan together for math and English language development. This evolution was supported by our data analysis. As we studied our data, it became clearer to us how we needed to broaden our planning efforts in a way that would improve our teaching.

We also needed to have a clear picture of how the planning should connect with the learning. So, we engaged in ghost walks, during which we visited each other's classrooms after school when the students were not there. We would enter, look at and read the room environment, and try to connect with the thinking, teaching, and learning based on the anchor charts the teachers were displaying.

The teachers began to realize why I was asking the questions I asked during the planning meetings. They understood how their planning had been disconnected. For example, they realized that they really did not have a mechanism to provide response to intervention. We really didn't have a pathway to connect with the bilingual teachers. They also realized that this was very complicated. They weren't connecting with student learning. It was more about covering discrete skills. So, it made sense to them that the climate and the culture were in a state of disconnect.

I tried to convey to them that I was here to support them. It took me about a year and a half to convince them that the vision was the right vision for our students and for each other. And so, now our brand is this very strong teacher collaboration model that is comprehensive. They work really hard, but I make sure that I'm nourishing them with food and praise, and promoting what's going on in classrooms.

The work they're engaged in is phenomenal. The depth of the conversations and the outcomes we're observing are strong indicators that the children are in a better place because of our efforts.

Olivia Amador-Valerio, Principal, Myrtle S. Finney
Elementary, Chula Vista, CA

The perception that "we can succeed" dramatically propels schools forward.

Leaders who influence outstanding results for all demographic groups help stakeholders believe they have abundant support and, consequently, abundant capacity to succeed. Students are willing to work hard and achieve remarkable academic results when they perceive they have multiple avenues for obtaining quality support (e.g., support from teachers, support from other school personnel, support for non-academic needs, study aids, tutoring, exemplar work samples, rubrics, technological tools, avenues for learning prerequisite skills, and no-risk opportunities to try new skills) that will help them succeed. Teachers are willing to pursue the lofty expectations of their administrators when they perceive they have everything they need to meet and exceed those expectations (e.g., training, materials, time, exemplar work samples, no-risk opportunities to try, feedback, technological support, peer support, and support for addressing students' non-academic needs).

In high-performing urban schools, a powerful surge of energy emerges each time a student, parent, teacher, or support provider concludes that they have the capacity to do whatever it takes to produce outstanding results. According to Bandura (1977), efficacy is the belief in one's capabilities to marshal the motivation, cognitive resources, and courses of action needed to successfully achieve expected outcomes. As mentioned in Chapter 5, the collective efficacy of a school team can be more powerful than socio-economic factors in predicting student achievement (Goddard, Hoy, & Hoy, 2000). The perception that "we can succeed" dramatically propels schools forward. As shared in the story at the beginning of this chapter, the principal at Finney Elementary in Chula Vista influenced the collective efficacy of her team. In virtually all of the high-performing urban schools we studied, leaders made conscientious, persistent efforts to build the efficacy of school personnel and promote a "we can succeed" transformational culture.

Efficacy, however, is situational. A team can feel quite effective in one setting and feel ineffective in another. For example, educators might feel efficacious when they teach well-behaved, middle-class, White students, who live with two college-educated parents, and who demonstrate thorough mastery of important prerequisite skills. The same team of educators might feel quite differently in a school where students who meet this description haven't enrolled in years. Leaders in urban schools may face a considerable challenge as they seek to influence a sense of collective efficacy. To bring about excellent and equitable learning results, leaders must provide a quantity and quality of support that helps stakeholders perceive that, together, they can and will succeed.

In the absence of high-quality support, human beings may not exert the requisite effort to achieve excellent and equitable learning results, even if they are convinced these results are desirable (see Chapter 5), they believe the results are attainable (see Chapter 6), and they know what they need to do to contribute to the attainment of the results (see Chapter 7). Only when individuals feel that they have a reasonable likelihood of success are they likely to engage fully and energetically in improvement efforts. Therefore, school leaders are challenged to create an environment within which educators perceive that they have the support they need to achieve what they have never previously achieved, for populations of students they have never served well, amidst all of the frustrations that typically confront urban schools, districts, and communities.

Bandura (1997) asserted that self-efficacy beliefs derive from four types of experiences: performance accomplishments, vicarious experiences, verbal persuasion, and psychological experiences. Tschannen-Moran and Gareis (2005) found that performance accomplishments, or mastery experiences, were particularly potent sources of self-efficacy beliefs in school settings. But, how does a leader build self-efficacy beliefs or the collective efficacy of school personnel in settings where successes have been rare? In schools where underperformance has been common and despair has established a foothold, how do leaders make a difference? In the high-performing schools we studied, leaders employed four strategies that helped them build the capacity of stakeholders to succeed and create a high level of both self-efficacy and collective efficacy. Specifically, leaders identified and addressed the reasons stakeholders did not undertake essential roles and responsibilities well. Leaders also developed platforms for the leadership of others in ways that maximized the support available to school personnel and other stakeholders. Critically, leaders provided enough support to reduce fear and magnify enthusiasm among all groups of stakeholders. And finally, leaders skillfully integrated professional development, collaborative planning, and observation and feedback in ways that built the capacity of educators to generate learning successes for all groups of students. While these four strategies are described separately in this chapter, in practice they are interwoven into the fabric of high-performing urban schools. Throughout the chapter, we broadly mention the importance of building the capacity of all stakeholders, including students and parents. For many school leaders, however, the most critical challenge is building the capacity of school personnel. For this reason, most of the examples provided in this chapter focus on the efforts leaders made to build capacity of teachers and other school personnel.

Identifying and Responding to the Reasons for the Lack of Effectiveness

As leaders begin working in typical urban schools, they often find many examples of ineffective, inefficient, and counter-productive behavior among students, parents, teachers, and other school personnel. Most principals, in the high-performing schools we studied, described how they encountered many examples of such ineffective, inefficient, and counter-productive behaviors when they began working at the schools they eventually helped transform. For example, principals talked about frequent hostile interactions between teachers and students; class sessions in which teachers lectured to students for the entire 80-minute block; collaborative planning meetings during which educators did not collaborate and did not plan; utilization of iPads and laptop computers as little more than electronic worksheets; report-card meetings in which parents and teachers blamed each other for every difficulty the student was encountering; the issuance of office referrals to students for their sarcastic and/or threatening looks; and many other ineffective, inefficient, and counter-productive behaviors.

In her comparative study of a NCUST award-winning school with a similar urban school in the same district, Manriquez (2012) found that many of the ineffective practices that were prevalent at both schools persisted at the comparison school and were eliminated in the school that achieved excellent and equitable learning results. The critical question, of course, considers how leaders in successful schools manage to minimize or eliminate the negative, ineffective practices. We have concluded that part of the answer rests squarely in the ways leaders built the capacity of students, parents, teachers, and other key stakeholders to work effectively, efficiently, and productively together. Fullan (2006) contended that turnaround leaders "assume that lack of capacity is the initial problem and work on it continuously" (p. 60). Leaders were able to build the capacity of their stakeholders, in large part, because of the leaders' mindset related to the individuals they encountered.

The Leader's Mindset Lens

In the high-performing urban schools we studied, leaders assumed that they could help stakeholders grow and succeed and leaders held themselves accountable for taking concrete actions to ensure everyone's success.

Dweck (2006) explained that many people have either a fixed mindset (believing that personal qualities are permanent) or a growth mindset (believing that personal qualities can be cultivated through effort). In many typical, struggling urban schools we see leaders who view students, parents, teachers, and support staff through the lens of a fixed mindset. They perceive that people are not likely to change, unless they are forced to change (and even forced changes are likely to be shallow and temporary). More specifically, leaders in schools that are not improving tend to perceive two overarching reasons for ineffective, inefficient, or counter-productive behavior:

1) The individual is insubordinate and does not want to change, or

2) The individual is incompetent and cannot change.

This mindset is reflected in statements such as "He knows what he should do, but he just doesn't care," "She is probably never going to be able to teach concepts that go beyond the textbook," "I can see him teaching basic math, but he'll never be a good Algebra II teacher," or "Let's be realistic. With her home situation, she's never going to do well in honors classes."

In contrast, leaders in high-performing urban schools often saw students, parents, teachers, and support staff through a growth-mindset lens. In describing growth-minded leaders, Dweck explained that "they start with a belief in human potential and development—both their own and other people's" (2006, p. 125). In the high-performing urban schools we studied, leaders assumed that they could help stakeholders grow and succeed and leaders held themselves accountable for taking concrete actions to ensure everyone's success. The principal at Myrtle S. Finney Elementary in Chula Vista did not assume that her team's early attempts at collaboration reflected their inability or unwillingness to implement the concept well. Instead, she recognized that they needed to better understand the reasons for collaborative planning teams, as well as the critical factors that would make them effective. Furthermore, the principal assumed that she had a responsibility for building the team's capacity to collaborate in ways that led to improved teaching and learning. The principal's actions reflected her growth mindset, both for her school personnel and for herself.

It is important to note that most of the high-performing schools leaders told stories about individuals that they were not able to help. They talked about students that they had to suspend in order to protect other students and/or teachers. They mentioned parents who they had to bar from campus. As well, they described situations where teachers and other school personnel were fired or convinced to leave. But, overwhelmingly, leaders exhibited the belief that individuals could change and improve with effort.

Learning Why People Do What They Do

Instead of assuming that growth was impossible or unlikely, leaders, in the high-performing schools studied, tried to better understand why they were seeing ineffective, inefficient, or counter-productive behaviors. At Franklin Elementary in Bakersfield, California the principal and instructional specialist frequently visited every classroom; however, they spent considerable time in the classrooms of teachers whose students did not perform well on the school's common formative assessments. The leaders attempted to understand why student performance was less than optimal, before they attempted to intervene.

In the high-performing urban schools, principals spent considerable time observing classrooms and debriefing with teachers. A leader at one high-performing high school in Los Angeles reflected on critical insights acquired during observations, as she both examined what was happening in the classroom and, simultaneously, thought about why the teacher might have said or done something that was less than effective, efficient, or productive. The leader explained:

> I went into a classroom of a teacher who was having lots of student behavior issues. She was referring lots of Latino and Black males to the office and we just don't do that here. The short of the story is that, by watching, I realized that she was afraid of the kids. She didn't push them to engage in the lessons. She let them do what they wanted, but when things got a little too loud, she quickly sent them to the office. So, we talked about her fears and we talked about how she could try to make more of a personal connection and get to know the students. I tried to be understanding of where she was, but I also tried to give her lots of ideas about how to structure a better situation. Anyway, it's a lot better now. She still has room for improvement, but she sends very few kids to the office and the kids like her more. The kids produce much more good work and they really are learning.

This story and many similar stories illustrate how principals utilized a growth-mindset lens as they worked with students, teachers, parents, and others. Instead of assuming that negative practices were the result of insubordination or incompetence, they invested time and effort to learn about the reasons that might have led to ineffective, inefficient, or counter-productive behaviors. For example, in some instances leaders learned that behaviors resulted from misunderstandings about expected practices, lack of knowledge about how to utilize available technology, discomfort with abandoning comfortable routines, fear of failing to implement a desired practice well, knowledge of only one way to teach a concept or skill, lack of in-depth understanding of a complex standard, fear of frustrating students by asking difficult questions, fear of straying from the textbook, concern that students might think the teacher was a racist, lack of comfort communicating to parents who might not speak English well, as well as many other reasons that could be addressed through quality support.

An assistant principal at MacArthur Senior High School in Houston's Aldine Independent School District explained the importance of asking teachers why they performed as they did, when the answer was not obvious. The assistant principal explained:

> Sometimes, I've sat in a classroom and I've been stunned to see a teacher still doing what I know we've talked about as a practice that just doesn't work for our students. So, I've learned to say, "We've talked several times about you doing *this*, but today, I observed you doing *this* [other behavior]." I'll ask them why they did what they did. I try not to ask in a negative way. I try to get them to see that I'm really trying to understand. For example, a couple of months ago, I asked a teacher, "Just before you asked those three low-level questions, what was in your mind? What were you thinking?" And a lot of times I'll get a very honest answer. That particular teacher told me, "I knew you were in here looking at my questioning strategies and I realized I had only asked a couple of questions, so I figured that I better ask some. But, I couldn't think of any really good ones that required a depth of understanding, so I just asked the first three things that came to mind." Her honest answer gave me a chance to talk with her about putting several good questions into each lesson plan. Later, without identifying the teacher, I shared the idea with the department team, so now when they meet to plan they work together to identify good questions they can use in each lesson.

Sharing Responsibility

Like the MacArthur Assistant Principal, leaders in the high-performing schools we studied shared responsibility for helping teachers and others succeed at meeting expectations. Carolyn Pugh, the principal at R.N. Harris Elementary in Durham, North Carolina, explained, "Yes, if you work here, it's your job to help all of our students succeed, but it's my job to help you succeed." Leaders assumed that they had a responsibility for building the capacity of people to perform essential roles and responsibilities well. Leaders embraced the spirit of Fullan's (2006) charge, "Capacity building first, and judgment second—because this is what will motivate more people" (p. 61).

Sharing responsibility for building capacity requires a major commitment of time and effort, especially in struggling schools where ineffective, inefficient, and counterproductive practices prevail. Leaders are not likely to build capacity by sitting in their offices, answering email, or completing reports. In the high-performing schools we studied, much of the capacity building occurred as leaders observed classrooms and provided constructive feedback; as they observed, participated in, and sometimes guided teacher collaboration meetings; as they listened to, counseled, and supported students and parents (both individually and in groups); and as they arranged for and provided professional development that was directly connected to classroom performances. This investment of time and effort signaled to stakeholders (teachers, parents, students, and other school personnel) the leader's sincere commitment to their success. These overt efforts to share responsibility for success inspired many stakeholders to redouble their efforts to improve their practices.

Distributing Leadership to Build Capacity

Principals in almost all of the high-performing schools we studied acted as if building capacity was too important a role to be contained solely in one position. In small schools, leaders found ways to create capacity-building responsibilities for teacher leaders. In large schools, leaders resisted the temptation to assign other administrators exclusively to traditional vice-principal roles (e.g., discipline, athletics, facilities, report writing) and, instead, insisted that those individuals fulfill major responsibilities related to building capacity in ways that would strengthen the positive transformational culture, improve access to challenging curricula, and ensure engaging, effective instruction for all students. The reality typically defies urban legend about heroic principals who demonstrated superhuman strength, wisdom, persistence, and courage as they lifted their schools to amazing accomplishments. While most of the schools we studied featured impressive principals, their success was influenced substantially by their ability to engage others in the hard work of building capacity. The principals distributed the practice of leadership (Spillane, 2006) in ways that built the capacity of stakeholders to create a coherent educational improvement system.

Spillane (2006) emphasized leadership as a practice or set of actions rather than a position or title. In high-performing urban schools, we found that leaders thoughtfully identified the leadership practices that were needed in order to build capacity and then identified the individuals who could assume such capacity-building responsibilities well. Additionally, principals were careful to provide support and guidance to the individuals who assumed the capacity-building responsibilities.

At MacArthur Senior High School in Houston's Aldine Independent School District, most of the school's assistant principals assumed responsibility for supporting teaching and learning in a curricular area. Assistant principals attended collaboration meetings, observed classrooms, provided feedback, and determined professional development needs. This work was carefully coordinated by the principal who met with assistant principals regularly to learn about challenges, evidences of growth, and plans of action. The distribution of leadership practice was similar in other large NCUST award-winning schools such as James Pace Early College High School in Brownsville, Texas; Revere High School near Boston, Massachusetts; and Mallard Creek High School in Charlotte, North Carolina.

Even in small, high-performing urban schools leaders found opportunities to engage and support others in providing leadership that built the capacity of others. Many of the schools utilized instructional specialists, literacy coaches, grade-level team leaders, counselors, and resource specialists to help enact a coherent educational improvement system focused on creating a positive transformational culture, challenging curricula, and engaging, effective instruction. For example, at Lauderbach Elementary in the Chula Vista Elementary School District, teacher leaders assumed responsibility for helping their colleagues design lessons that had a high likelihood of guiding all students to mastery of specific, challenging academic standards.

It is difficult to imagine how the high-performing urban schools we studied could have accomplished such major changes in culture, curricula, and instruction without the wise use of a team of leaders. By distributing and coordinating leadership tasks, principals ensured that teachers had sufficient access to high-quality support. Teachers and other school personnel were more likely to perceive a sense of efficacy, because there were easy-to-access colleagues who possessed 1) the knowledge and skills to help them succeed, 2) the ability to create a culture in which growth was likely, and 3) a sincere commitment to helping them succeed. A teacher at Signal Hill Elementary in Long Beach explained:

> This is such a team here. We get great support from the principal, but we also get great support from our fellow teachers. At this school, when teachers have leadership roles, they don't try to rule you. Instead, they try to help you succeed. It's so sincere that it makes you try even harder.

Similarly, a teacher at Highland Park Elementary in Silver Spring, Maryland stated:

> Our current principal and our last principal were both outstanding. They really knew how to help you teach. But, I really think we have accomplished so much because we also have amazing help from our fellow teachers. I'm amazed at how much they know. You can see it in their teaching. You can see it in the work their kids produce. And, they don't make it an ego thing. They just want to help other teachers here reach the same results. That's why this is an amazing school.

Providing Enough Support to Reduce Fear and Magnify Enthusiasm

Adopting a new practice often requires individuals to relinquish a more familiar or comfortable practice. This risk taking necessitates trust. Unfortunately, many leaders fail to build capacity in others (even when they try), because they fail to recognize the centrality of trust and the importance of reducing fear as individuals seek to improve. Building trust can be particularly challenging in situations when the leader confronts performances that are counter-productive to school goals (Robinson, 2011). While facing many tough situations, in the high-performing urban schools studied, leaders exhibited skill in building relationships and sustaining relationships that reduced fear, produced trust, and magnified enthusiasm for growing and improving.

As mentioned in Chapter 5, Tschannen-Moran (2014) explained that five facets of behavior influenced the development of trust: benevolence, honesty, openness, reliability, and competence. In interviews with teachers, administrators, and other school personnel, we heard many indications that leaders in high-performing urban schools exemplified these five facets as they sought to build the capacity of their teams.

Benevolence

It's not what you're doing to document. It's what you're doing to help them succeed.

In the high-performing urban schools studied, leaders convinced school personnel that they had two related purposes: 1) to support school personnel in ensuring the success of their students, and 2) to support school personnel in ensuring their own professional success. Administrators exhibited their positive, benevolent intentions consistently and regularly. For example, Rose Longoria, the principal at James Pace Early College High School in Brownsville, explained that she and her administrative team believed that "It's not what you're doing to document. It's what you're doing to help them succeed." More importantly, teachers and other school personnel reported that they believed that their leaders had positive intentions related to the success of their students and their own professional success. In interviews with Pace teachers, we heard several confirm, "The administrators here are determined to help us succeed."

In many interviews across the schools studied, teachers affirmed their perception that administrators and teacher leaders were determined to help them succeed professionally. For example, a teacher at Branch Brook Elementary in Newark, New Jersey explained the nature of interactions with the school administrator at her school.

> I've worked at other schools in this district where you didn't know what was going to happen when an administrator opened the door. You didn't know what their agenda was, so you just tensed up and tried to stay on the straight and narrow. Here, it's so completely different. It's weird because expectations here are higher than at any other school where I've taught. But, when the door opens and the principal enters, you know that his first priority is to help.

Repeatedly, school personnel emphasized that their leaders were primarily concerned with students and student learning. "Here, it is all about the kids, all of the kids," commented a teacher at R. N. Harris Elementary in Durham, North Carolina. A teacher at Escontrias Elementary in El Paso's Socorro Independent School District expressed a similar sentiment by relating the following:

> When the new principal came, this school had a bad reputation. They called this Escontrias ISD [Independent School District] because we acted like we were the district. When the new principal came, we all wore our union shirts just to let her know who we were. But, she came in with such a sincere focus on the kids. How could you argue against that? She changed everything by being so focused on helping the children, the families, and the community.

Teachers provided many examples of how their principals and other school leaders framed difficult feedback so that teachers perceived the feedback as supportive. For example, a teacher at Dr. Charles Lunsford School in Rochester, New

York explained how one of the school administrators provided feedback after an observation of a less than stellar lesson:

> I was new here and I was new to teaching. I was petrified each time one of the administrators came into my classroom. After one horrible lesson, one of the administrators whispered to me as she left the classroom, "Let's talk for a few minutes before you go home today." I thought I might be going home for good. When we met, she started the conversation by asking me what I had hoped to get the kids to understand during the lesson she observed. When I told her, she said, "Oh, that makes sense! That's a good learning goal." Then she asked me how many of the students did I think really learned what I was trying to teach and I honestly answered that maybe two or three got it. Then, I'll never forget what she said. She just said, "You know, I can help you with that. I can help you get almost all of your kids to master that concept tomorrow. I know you can do it and I know I can help you." Then she asked if I was willing to work with her. That's how I started here. Now, I think I'm a pretty good teacher. All of my students achieved proficiency in math last year.

Honesty and Openness

Leaders in high-performing schools also reduced fear through their honest, frank conversations about important issues. Teachers and other school personnel did not shy away from critical issues that influenced culture, curricula, and instruction. Teachers at many high-performing schools reported that they appreciated honest feedback from their leaders. For example, a teacher at Signal Hill Elementary in Long Beach, California reported:

> It's nice to know that you're getting the straight scoop about what administrators are thinking. In some schools, you hear nice things, but then later, you find out that the principal has serious concerns about your work. At Signal Hill, we [the teachers] know what the principal is thinking. There isn't mystery about what is important to her. She tells you what's going well and she tells you what she's concerned about.

Also, leaders did not shy away from critical concerns related to race, language background, socio-economic status, gender, or other variables. A teacher at Bursch Elementary in Compton explained why she perceived that honest conversations about difficult issues contributed to positive environment. She explained:

> At some schools, everyone knows what is going on, but nobody wants to address it directly. People know which students are not being taught, but nobody says anything or they focus on other things that aren't the real issue. Here it is refreshing because we can talk about issues of race and language in an open and honest way. The principal just speaks honestly and challenges us to think about what we need to do to reach every one of our students.

It is important to note that honesty and openness occurred in a context of benevolence.

Reliability

As mentioned in Chapter 2, a teacher at Horace Mann Elementary in Glendale, CA exclaimed, "If the principal hasn't been in my classroom for a day or two, I want to find out what's wrong!" Throughout the high-performing urban schools we studied, school personnel knew they could rely upon their principals for support. Dependability and reliability strengthened trust and collective efficacy. A teacher at Eastwood Middle School in El Paso's Ysleta Independent School District explained:

> There are a few things you can count on here. One is that the administrators here care about the kids and they care about the staff. Second is that they show they care by being visible in classrooms, in hallways, all day, every day. Third is that they're positive. They share their concerns in a positive way, but they aren't afraid to tell you when you're doing something right.

Other teachers noted that their leaders dependably and reliably focused attention on the progress being achieved by all students and all groups of students. A teacher at Kearny School of International Business in San Diego asserted:

> You can be sure that when she [the principal] enters the door, she's looking to see what's going on with the kids. She wants to see who is engaged in the lesson and who is not, who understands what they're supposed to be learning and who is tuned out. She expects you to connect with all of them [the students], each one of them, regardless of ethnicity or language. You don't have to guess what's important to her. You can count on it.

Similarly, a teacher at Jim Thorpe Fundamental Academy in Santa Ana explained:

> This is a big school, but still the principal knows all of the kids. She knows which students have IEPs. She knows which ones are English learners. She'll ask, "What's your plan to engage this student more in conversation concerning the objective?" Or she'll ask, "How are you and the special education teacher working together to get this student to master this objective?"

By reliably focusing on the same major goals over time, leaders ensured that school personnel were not left guessing about the leader's priorities. School personnel could trust that yesterday's focal points of improvement efforts would continue to be focal points tomorrow and next month, and (perhaps, with some fine adjustments) even next year. Teachers were less likely to wonder if "this idea would soon pass" and more likely to believe that there was an overarching, compelling vision about how the school would achieve excellent and equitable learning results.

Finally, it is important to note that perceptions of reliability were enhanced by leadership stability. In the high-performing schools we studied, school personnel benefited from consistent leadership. Often principals had four or more years of experience at the school, so educators knew what to expect. In the schools that sustained a positive growth trajectory subsequent to a principal transition, the incoming principal espoused the same or similar priorities, recognized and supported the successful practices teachers had adopted, and sought to strengthen and deepen those practices, rather than start anew with a different set of priorities and initiatives.

Competence

Principals built platforms for the leadership of individuals who knew how to educate the diverse groups of students they served.

In the high-performing schools studied, leaders successfully built the capacity of their school personnel, because school personnel perceived that the individuals providing leadership were highly competent. School personnel perceived that the administrators and teacher leaders who served them possessed the requisite knowledge and skills to assist them in improving learning results for all the students they served.

A teacher at Magnet Traditional School in Phoenix, Arizona shared that her principal "always adds value to our instructional practice." A teacher at Highland Park Elementary in Silver Spring, Maryland explained, "We have the benefit of learning from and with real experts in curriculum and instruction. You can see results quickly by following their advice." A teacher at Horace Mann Dual Language Magnet in Wichita, Kansas exclaimed, "We get coached by the very best educational leaders! They know two-way bilingual instruction as well as anybody." A teacher at Southside Elementary in Miami-Dade County, Florida described the instructional leaders at her school by saying, "First, what they say makes sense for the kids we serve, primarily English learners. Second, you see the results in the data. You know that they [the school leaders] aren't just philosophers. They're educators."

Perceptions of confidence were enhanced, not diminished, by the distribution of leadership practices throughout the high-performing urban schools. Principals looked for, hired, promoted, and/or positioned individuals who had the expertise necessary to build the capacity of school personnel to accomplish the critical roles and responsibilities that were essential to the school's success. Principals built platforms for the leadership of individuals who knew how to educate the diverse groups of students they served. Even after principals positioned these teacher leaders/administrators, principals worked continuously to support them in ways that continued to build their capacity to build the capacity of other school personnel.

Also, perceptions of competence were grounded in data. By focusing on data, especially data from common formative assessments or short-cycle assessments, leaders were able to help educators see validation of their efforts to improve culture, curricula, and instruction. Datnow and Park (2014) emphasized how teachers and administrators in their study used a broad array of data beyond end-of-year state assessments. They explained:

> These examples [including course placement trends, formative assessments, and observations of both student and teacher behaviors] reinforce that the process of examining data can propel positive changes in classroom practices—a process that requires reflecting on both data and existing instructional practices. (p. 101)

In the high-performing urban schools we studied, leaders were able to accelerate their capacity-building efforts by helping teachers generate small learning successes that were visible in their own student data. "The proof is in the pudding," explained a teacher at Escontrias Elementary in El Paso's Socorro Independent School District. She continued, "When you see in the data that what the principal suggested is helping your students learn content they never learned before, you become a believer."

By focusing on evidence of student learning, leaders also demonstrated their ability to help teachers succeed with all of the diverse populations they were assigned to teach. Leaders in the high-performing urban schools were able to help school personnel find evidence in their own student data that they could lead all students to academic success.

Integrating Collaboration, Professional Development, and Observation and Feedback

The principal at Myrtle S. Finney Elementary in Chula Vista successfully built the capacity of her school personnel by deliberately integrating collaboration, professional development, and observation and feedback. The principal recognized that she needed to broaden and deepen collaboration efforts, but she also knew that teachers required appropriate professional development to help them understand what quality collaboration entailed. She knew that she had to find ways to help teachers see the connection between their collaborative planning and the work they did inside their classrooms, so the principal found ways to utilize observation and feedback (starting first with "ghost walks") so teachers came to understand how key concepts fit together to influence student learning.

Similarly, many other leaders in the high-performing urban schools studied linked teacher collaboration, professional development, and classroom observation and feedback in ways that improved the initial instruction provided to all students, but also in ways that improved the quality and effectiveness of intervention and enrichment efforts.

Hargreaves and Fullan (2012, p. 88) proposed that attention to professional capital was "essential for transforming the teaching profession into a force for the common good." They explained that, in the context of schools, professional capital was the confluence of human capital (the critical knowledge and skills that teachers must possess), social capital (the quantity and quality of social interactions that increase the extent to which teachers possess the critical knowledge and skills), and decisional capital (the ability to make effective decisions about teaching).

Our findings support the importance of professional capital. In the high-performing urban schools we studied, leaders endeavored to hire or acquire the best (most knowledgeable and skillful) teachers they could find, while further building human capital by providing frequent observations and quality feedback. As well, they enhanced human capital by providing intensive, job-embedded professional development that was tightly connected to the issues they observed when visiting classrooms. Importantly, leaders also sought to build social capital and decisional capital by engaging all teachers in frequent collaborations, focused on improving instruction. Human capital (teachers' knowledge and skill) increased over time as teachers engaged with, and learned from, their peers. As they addressed the primary concerns that emerged from regular classroom observations, and applied knowledge and skills learned through professional development offerings, they increased their ability to make decisions that resulted in all students (and all groups of students) mastering important academic content. The integration of collaboration, professional development, and observation and feedback nurtured professional capital in high-performing urban schools.

In the high-performing schools, teacher collaboration, professional development, and observation and feedback were not separate, random acts of administration. For example, at Southside Elementary in Miami-Dade County, teachers benefitted from rich professional development in object-based or experiential learning. This professional development was enhanced and deepened by weekly teacher collaboration sessions during which teachers used the knowledge they had acquired to plan strong lessons that were likely to lead the school's diverse learners to mastery of important concepts. As well, the plans developed as a result of the collaboration were further reinforced as school leaders observed classrooms and offered feedback, noting the degree to which implemented lessons were engaging students and maximizing their learning. Additionally, classroom observations helped leaders identify ways in which subsequent professional development could be of additional benefit as teachers endeavored to refine and improve implementation.

Summary

Leaders who want their schools to produce excellent and equitable learning results face the challenge of building the capacity of their stakeholders to succeed. If school personnel do not perceive that they have the quantity and quality of support they need in order to help their diverse students succeed academically, success is unlikely.

In the high-performing schools we studied, leaders built the individual and collective capacity of stakeholders by employing four strategies. First, utilizing a growth mindset (rather than a fixed mindset), leaders identified and responded to the reasons school personnel did not address essential roles and responsibilities well. Leaders assumed that improvement was possible, and leaders shared responsibility for helping school personnel grow and improve.

Second, leaders distributed leadership responsibilities and practices in ways that maximized the support available to school personnel and other stakeholders. In larger schools, leaders gave assistant principals, other administrators, and teacher leaders responsibilities for supporting and building the capacity of school personnel. Even in smaller schools with only one administrator, principals created opportunities for teacher leaders to support and build the capacity of their colleagues.

Next, leaders provided enough support to reduce fear and magnify enthusiasm among all groups of stakeholders. In particular, leaders built trust by establishing their positive, student-focused intentions, interacting honestly and openly, demonstrating reliability and dependability, and by exhibiting professional competence. And, finally, leaders skillfully integrated professional development, collaborative planning, and observation and feedback in ways that built the capacity of educators to generate learning successes for all groups of students.

What It Is & What It Isn't: Leadership that Builds Capacity to Succeed

What It Is: Demonstrating a Growth Mindset

When the school leader enters a classroom and finds ineffective practices, the leader immediately starts thinking, "What does this educator need to know, see, or experience that would help them successfully implement more effective practices?" The leader assumes that growth is possible, and even likely with the right support.

What It Isn't: Demonstrating a Fixed Mindset

When the school leader enters a classroom and finds ineffective practices, the leader immediately starts thinking, "How can I get rid of this person? Or, if I can't get rid of the person, how can I place them where they will do minimal harm?" The leader assumes that growth is impossible or unlikely.

*   *   *

What It Is: Learning Why People Do What They Do

When the school leader enters a classroom and finds ineffective practices, the leader immediately starts thinking, "Why is she doing what she's doing? What is she trying to accomplish? What is she trying to avoid?" If the answers aren't clear, the leader finds ways to ask the teacher directly.

What It Isn't: Assuming Incompetence or Insubordination

When the school leader enters a classroom and finds ineffective practices, the leader immediately starts thinking, "He's doing this, even though he knows better." The leader assumes that the educator is either incompetent or insubordinate.

*   *   *

What It Is: Sharing Responsibility for the Success of School Personnel

When the school leader enters a classroom and finds ineffective practices, the leader immediately starts thinking, "What will I need to do in order to ensure that this person successfully changes ineffective practices?" The leader assumes that he or she has a responsibility for helping the educator succeed.

What It Isn't: Shaming and Blaming Personnel without Personal Responsibility

When the school leader enters a classroom and finds ineffective practices, the leader immediately starts thinking, "How can I write this up so that this person knows that they aren't going to be successful in this school?" The leader assumes that his or her job is to report, not to support.

*   *   *

What It Is: Distributing Leadership in Ways that Build Capacity

The school leader ensures that a variety of qualified individuals share responsibilities for building the capacity of school personnel to assume critical roles well. Even when funds are limited, the school leader finds ways to create platforms for the leadership of others. The school leader provides support, guidance, mentoring, and evaluation for the individuals who share leadership responsibility, so that school personnel perceive that they have access to abundant, high-quality support.

What It Isn't: Restricting Leadership to the Principal's Office

The school leader assumes that he or she is the only available, qualified, or appropriate person to support school personnel. In large schools, other administrators are assigned duties that are tangential to the goals of improving culture, curricula, and instruction. In small schools, the principal does not support teachers or other personnel in assuming leadership responsibilities.

* * *

What It Is: Demonstrating Benevolent Intent

When the school leader consults with a teacher who consistently utilizes ineffective practices, the teacher assumes that the leader's primary intent is to help students learn and succeed and the leader's secondary intent is to help the teacher succeed in helping students learn. The teacher makes this assumption, because the leader deliberately communicates these intentions consistently and sincerely.

What It Isn't: Making Intent Unclear

When the school leader consults with a teacher who consistently utilizes ineffective practices, the teacher assumes that the leader's primary intent is to document the teacher's poor performance and pursue disciplinary action. The teacher makes this assumption, at least in part, because the leader does not communicate any other intent in a consistent and sincere manner.

* * *

What It Is: Interacting Honestly, Openly, and Reliably

When the school leader consults with a teacher who consistently utilizes ineffective practices, the teacher perceives the leader as honest, open, and reliable. The teacher makes this assumption because the leader shares both strengths and weaknesses, acknowledges improvements, and offers consistent, dependable support.

What It Isn't: Being Unpredictable

When the school leader consults with a teacher who consistently utilizes ineffective practices, the teacher is suspicious of the leader, in part because the leader seems to focus only on evidence that supports negative contentions. If the teacher refutes the leader's contention, the leader comes up with another negative contention with additional negative evidence; or, at times, the leader curiously drops negative contentions and seems to act as if the observation went well, when the teacher is relatively certain that the leader is just seeking to avoid a tense moment.

* * *

What It Is: Demonstrating Competence and Inspiring Confidence

When the school leader consults with a teacher who consistently utilizes ineffective practices, the teacher assumes that the leader is a competent educator who has the ability and the desire to help him or her help students learn and succeed. The teacher makes this assumption because the leader does not simply highlight what is not working (i.e., "Here is the list of things you did not do well"). Instead, the leader helps the teacher know how to change his or her practice through opportunities to learn about a more effective practice, understand some of the research or evidence that supports the practice, see the practice in action, try the practice with support, receive feedback and support, and try again. The leader helps the teacher collect and review his or her student data that highlight how learning results improve as implementation of the practice improves.

What It Isn't: Compliance and Power

When the school leader consults with a teacher who consistently utilizes ineffective practices, the teacher doubts that the leader knows how to help him or her help students learn and succeed. The teacher makes this assumption, because sometimes the leader is able to tell the teacher what is ineffective (i.e., "Here is the list of things you did not do well"), but the leader is unable to offer the teacher any useful assistance in moving from the ineffective practice to a more effective practice. The teacher also doubts that the leader knows how to help him or her because the leader makes statements or puts forth expectations that do not have the support of research or best-practice evidence. Often, the teacher perceives that the leader's requests are nothing more than busy work or a popular fad, largely because the leader is unable to explain the rationale behind the requested practice. The leader gives little attention to whether or not students are learning important content. Attention is focused, instead, on whether or not the teacher is complying with the leader's requests.

* * *

What It Is: Building Coherence

School personnel perceive that their professional development experiences at school, their collaborative planning, and the observations and feedback they receive from leaders are tightly coupled. Teachers believe that they are focused on a small number (perhaps two or three) of key issues related to the improvement of teaching and learning. They see those issues at the core of what they are learning in professional development sessions. At the same time, they see those issues as focal points in their collaborative planning with colleagues. And, when school leaders visit their classrooms, those same issues are the focus of constructive feedback.

What It Isn't: Sustaining Incoherence

School personnel see little or no connection between their professional development experiences at school, their collaborative planning, and the observations and feedback they receive from leaders. When teachers are asked to name the key issues that are the focus of improvement efforts at their school, they provide a long list of priorities and programs, citing different professional development initiatives, different tasks they complete during collaborative planning, and different themes that tend to come from the observations and feedback provided by school leaders. Ultimately, teachers do not know what they are expected to do well, or they just assume that they are expected to do everything.

School Self-Assessment Tool: Does Your School Leadership Build Capacity to Succeed?

This self-assessment will help you determine the extent to which leadership at your school builds capacity to succeed. Consider engaging teams of teachers, administrators, parents, and students to respond to these questions. (One could invite participants to provide individual ratings and then compile separate ratings for stakeholder groups.) Completion of the self-assessment will generate a picture of the school's current practices. By utilizing the same process annually or semi-annually, the school community can assess progress in influencing the desire to change. Rate the following on a scale of 1 to 5, with 1 representing NOT LIKELY and 5 representing VERY LIKELY.

I. How likely is it that school personnel perceive that their leaders have a growth mindset related to their ability to teach their students well? How likely is it that school personnel perceive that their leaders believe that they possess the ability to improve teaching and learning for their students? Rating _____

If different groups of school personnel would be likely to respond to this item differently, explain to what extent responses would vary and why: _____

II. When school leaders encounter ineffective teaching practices, how likely is it that leaders strive to understand the reasons the teacher utilizes the practice and the reasons the teacher has not adopted a more effective practice? Rating _____

If different groups of school personnel would be likely to respond to this item differently, explain to what extent responses would vary and why: _____

III. When school leaders encounter ineffective teaching practices, how likely is it that teachers perceive that the leader shares responsibility for helping the teacher adopt a more effective practice? Rating

_____

If different groups of school personnel would be likely to respond to this item differently, explain to what extent responses would vary and why: _____

IV. How likely is it that school personnel perceive that they have abundant sources of leadership and support that build their capacity to ensure the academic success of all their students? Rating _____

If different groups of school personnel would be likely to respond to this item differently, explain to what extent responses would vary and why: _____

V. When school leaders identify ineffective teaching practices, how likely is it that teachers will assume that the leader's primary intent is to help students learn and succeed and the leader's secondary intent is to help the teacher succeed in helping students learn? Rating

_____

If different groups of school personnel would be likely to respond to this item differently, explain to what extent responses would vary and why: _____

VI. When school leaders confer with teachers about ineffective teaching practices, how likely is it that teachers will assume that the leader is honest, open, and reliable in providing feedback and support intended to help the teacher improve? Rating _____

If different groups of school personnel would be likely to respond to this item differently, explain to what extent responses would vary and why: _____

VII. When school leaders confer with teachers about ineffective teaching practices, how likely is it that teachers will assume that the leader is a competent educator who has the ability and the desire to help him or her help students learn and succeed? Rating _____

If different groups of school personnel would be likely to respond to this item differently, explain to what extent responses would vary and why: _____

VIII. How likely is it that school personnel perceive that professional development activities, collaborative planning work, and the observation and feedback they receive from school leaders are all focused on the same few central issues? Rating _____

If different groups of school personnel would be likely to respond to this item differently, explain to what extent responses would vary and why: _____

References

Bandura, A. (1977). Self-efficacy: Toward a unifying theory of behavioral change. *Psychological Review, 84*, 191–215.

Bandura, A. (1997). *Self-efficacy: The exercise of control.* New York: W. H. Freeman & Company.

Datnow, A., & Park, V. (2014). *Data-driven leadership.* San Francisco, CA: Jossey-Bass.

Dweck, C. S. (2006). *Mindset: The new psychology of success.* New York: Ballantine Books.

Fullan, M. (2006). *Turnaround leadership.* San Francisco, CA: Jossey-Bass.

Goddard, R. D., Hoy, W. K., & Hoy, A. W. (2000). Collective teacher efficacy: Its meaning, measure, and effect on student achievement. *American Education Research Journal, 37*(2), 479–507.

Hargreaves, A., & Fullan, M. (2012). *Professional capital: Transforming teaching in every school.* New York: Teachers College Press.

Manriquez, C. (2012). *Turnaround schools: A comparative case study of two small schools.* D.Ed. dissertation, San Diego State University.

Robinson, V. (2011). *Student-centered leadership.* San Francisco, CA: Jossey-Bass.

Spillane, J. P. (2006). *Distributed leadership.* San Francisco, CA: Jossey-Bass.

Tschannen-Moran, M. (2014). *Trust matters: Leadership in successful schools*, 2nd ed. San Francisco, CA: Jossey-Bass.

Tschannen-Moran, M., & Gareis, C. (2005, November). *Cultivating principals' sense of efficacy: Supports that matter.* Paper presented at the annual meeting of the University Council for Educational Administration, Nashville, TN.

Epilogue

Data from over 100 elementary, middle, and high schools from across the nation demonstrate that urban schools can achieve multiple evidences of high academic achievement for all of the diverse populations they serve. Urban schools that do not resort to selective admissions criteria are attaining excellent and equitable learning results. Most of the schools we identified and studied were traditional public schools that enrolled students in their neighborhoods. Some were public charter schools that enrolled students on a first-come, first-served or a lottery basis.

Equity and Excellence are Attainable

While we acknowledge that fiscal resources can make an important difference, we note that excellent and equitable results are being attained at schools that do not receive more fiscal resources than their sister schools in the same district and sometimes in the same neighborhood. While we acknowledge the important value that parents offer, we have heard parents tell us about the dramatic changes in learning their children experienced when they moved from one school to the high-performing school we awarded and studied. We believe that our nation can and should be dedicated to providing a much stronger web of support that ensures the physical, social, and emotional health and wellbeing of every child. However, we acknowledge that there are urban schools achieving impressive learning results for students, even when community supports are lacking. Clearly, the quality of schooling makes a profound difference to children's educational success. In fact, the quality of schooling may make an even greater difference for Black, Latino, and Native American children, children who live in low-income communities, children in foster care, children who have a first language other than English, children experiencing homelessness, children with disabilities, and other groups who have traditionally not been served well in schools.

The Pursuit of Excellence and Equity is Difficult

The evidence also suggests that the attainment of excellent and equitable learning results is difficult. We have not yet interviewed a principal who told us it was easy to turn around an urban school in a way that resulted in excellent and equitable learning results. Instead, we heard many stories about frustrations, disappointments, setbacks, and failures. Even school leaders who replaced turnaround leaders reported challenges as they sought to sustain the positive momentum created by their predecessors.

Perhaps the greatest evidence of the depth and breadth of challenges associated with creating high-performing urban schools is the relatively small number we find each year. We note, however, that each year, we encounter thousands of dedicated teachers and leaders who have a sincere commitment to improving their craft and creating outstanding schools. We see these educators yearning for the successes achieved in the schools we have studied, but they are frustrated.

We conclude that a major source of frustration derives from our profession's tendency to equip leaders with tools that might be helpful for tinkering with small refinements to practices, while societal expectations for student learning are growing substantially, at the same time the diversity of the children and families served by schools pose great challenges and opportunities. Too often, school leaders receive training and support for small incremental changes that require what Argyris and Schön (1974) referred to as single-loop learning. Single-loop learning involves implementing actions designed to conform with existing goals, values, plans, and rules. Single-loop learning often results in first-order changes that utilize known strategies to reduce deviation from the norm (Argyris, Putnam, & Smith, 1985). With single-loop learning in schools, leaders use first-order changes to ensure that classrooms are staffed, books are on the shelves, disciplinary policies are upheld, and courses are provided in ways consistent with norms that have existed for decades, using solutions that worked in the past.

In contrast, Argyris and Schön (1974) also defined double-loop learning. Double-loop learning addresses problems that require the establishment of new goals and values through the use of new thinking and new tools. When confronted with double-loop learning challenges, school leaders must consider what goals should drive educational efforts, who needs to be served well, and what should be new norms for defining quality. Argyris et al. (1985) explained that double-loop learning results in second-order changes where the system itself undergoes fundamental transformation. Second-order change requires leadership that can transform systems in response to new goals, norms, and expectations. Our educational systems tend to equip school leaders with first-order change tools (incremental change strategies based on what worked in the past) and then expect them to tackle second-order change challenges (deep changes to structures and systems to address new goals and values).

Where we found leaders who helped their schools achieve excellent and equitable learning results, the leaders realized that single-loop learning would not be sufficient for the second-order change that was required to lead all students to high levels of academic success. The solutions leaders needed could not be purchased in a textbook, a computer program, or a supplemental educational service. They realized that they would not achieve the results they wanted by simply attending a workshop, providing a web-based intervention, or sending school personnel to a class. They recognized that they had to change the essence of what was being taught in classrooms, so that curricula aligned with high academic standards (standards comparable to what is taught to students in more affluent schools). They recognized that they had to change how educators conceptualized the nature of effective instruction, so that instruction would result in all of the diverse populations of students served engaging deeply in, and actually demonstrating mastery of, the content. They recognized that they even had to change the climate and culture of the schools so that students, parents, and school personnel felt valued, appreciated, and supported. They had to create cultures in which individuals were likely to perceive that the institution was committed to their individual and collective success. In short, the leaders we studied understood the essence of the second-order changes they needed in order to attain excellent and equitable learning results for all students.

We also came to understand that leaders in the high-performing urban schools recognized that in order to create and sustain the needed changes to culture, curricula, and instruction, they had to build a coherent system of educational improvement. Even though many tasks had to be accomplished, leaders seemed to understand that everyone involved had to perceive that the changes were logical, reasonable, and doable.

Instead of asking people to embrace complex, multi-dimensional, abstract concepts, theories, and approaches, leaders convinced their stakeholders that they could make progress by agreeing upon the major concepts and ideas students should be expected to learn at each step along their educational journey and by committing to ensure that all children would learn those concepts and ideas. They also realized that if they were committing to ensure that all children learned the concepts, they needed both clarity and consistency regarding how educators would determine whether or not students were making progress learning those concepts (not just at the end of the year, but during the year, as students were being taught). Very importantly, leaders had to engage stakeholders in building a variety of linked structures to help teachers produce and implement outstanding lessons that were likely to result in all students demonstrating mastery of the key concepts when those concepts were initially taught. In other words, leaders created or utilized collaborative planning, professional development, and classroom observation and feedback structures to help teachers consistently develop lessons that resulted in diverse groups of students mastering challenging academic curricula. Also, leaders recognized how those same collaborative planning, professional development, and classroom observation and feedback structures needed to ensure the development, implementation, and ongoing improvement of intervention (when students needed additional support) and enrichment (when students could benefit from opportunities to deepen and integrate their understandings). Finally, leaders realized that none of these systemic outcomes would likely be achieved unless the system simultaneously resulted in students, parents, and school personnel perceiving that they were valued and capable.

Additionally, leaders in the high-performing urban schools studied recognized that they could not institute second-order changes by themselves. They had to depend upon the combined effort of a critical mass of stakeholders in order to have any real hope of attaining the cultural, curricular, and instructional changes that would drive the attainment of excellent and equitable learning results. Furthermore, they realized that getting people to change practices, habits, routines, policies, and structures was not easy for a multitude of reasons.

People were not likely to change unless they perceived that they were being asked to change for compelling reasons. Students were not willing to exert the effort required to master challenging academic standards if they perceived that educators were setting them up for more failure experiences. Parents were not willing to push their children to succeed if the parents were not convinced that educators had their children's best interest at heart. Teachers were not willing to exert the additional time and energy to teach challenging academic standards if they perceived that the only reason to do so was to improve performance on state tests they did not value.

Also, people were not likely to change unless they believed that success was attainable. Students had to perceive that, through their hard work, they would have a high likelihood of success both in school and beyond school. Parents who had experienced their own academic failure (sometimes in the same schools their children attended) had to be convinced that the school personnel who served their children had both the commitment and the ability to ensure their child's success. Teachers had to come to believe that their students could achieve important academic success; otherwise, it might be fruitless to exert the effort required to change.

Beyond accepting the reasons for change and embracing the belief that success was attainable, individuals had to understand their roles and responsibilities in bringing about the necessary changes. Students needed to understand their role in contributing to their academic success (e.g., practicing good study habits, rereading content, asking clarifying questions). Parents needed to know how they played a supportive role in ensuring their children's academic success (e.g., reinforcing positive social and academic behavior, encouraging children to talk about the concepts they were learning, promoting recreational reading). And, of course, school personnel needed to know and understand the aspects of their roles that had the greatest influence on getting students (especially diverse populations of students) to excel academically (e.g., building positive teacher–student relationships, providing clarity, teaching to mastery, providing quality feedback).

Finally, stakeholders had to perceive that they had a sufficient quality and quantity of support so that they had a reasonable likelihood of experiencing success. In order to risk the time, energy, and ego connected with pursuing fundamental, second-order change, students, parents, and school personnel had to perceive that they had enough support to win. Students and parents needed to see that they had enough support to break out of cycles of failure and frustration. School personnel needed to feel a collective efficacy: a sense that they were a team that had the capacity to ensure that their students would achieve impressive academic gains. As well, school personnel needed to believe that they were valuable members of the team who made significant contributions to the organization's accomplishments.

As leaders acquired and acted upon their understanding of the changes needed, improvements occurred. The changes took time (often three, four, or five years in order to generate substantial differences in academic learning results). Progress was often uneven, with spurts of growth, stalls, areas of impressive progress, and even some major mid-course corrections. Nonetheless, successes were achieved. Children in some of the nation's poorest communities demonstrated proficiency on challenging academic standards at higher rates than the overall proficiency rates for their states. Course completion rates, success in advanced courses, attendance rates, college entrance exam scores, and many other measures increased dramatically. Whereas many of their parents and older siblings dropped out of school, the children served in these high-performing schools graduated (or are en route to graduating) well prepared for college, post-secondary education programs, and careers. These successes should inspire us to look deeply into our educational systems and determine how we can make the attainment of excellent and equitable learning results commonplace throughout our nation. As mentioned in Chapter 1, Paul Batalden wrote, "Every system is perfectly designed to get the results it gets" (Carr, 2008). How can we perfectly redesign our systems so that we achieve excellent and equitable learning results for all of our nation's children?

Implications for School Leader Preparation

As universities, school districts, and other committed partners work together to improve school leader preparation, scholars and practitioners should be clear about the goals they intend to pursue in helping leadership candidates achieve. If programs do not intend to prepare leaders to pursue excellent and equitable learning results, they should clearly articulate their intents. Alternately, if they intend to prepare leaders to serve diverse populations of students and families well, preparation programs need to identify and commit to the essential second-order changes they must institute in order to prepare leaders to bring about second-order changes in public schools.

School leader preparation programs should utilize the knowledge available from studies of high-performing urban schools to specify the knowledge, skills, and dispositions today's school leaders should demonstrate if they are likely to address leadership challenges in ways that bring about positive transformational cultures, access to challenging curricula, and engaging, effective instruction for all students. Not only should preparation programs begin the iterative process of identifying, testing, and refining notions about the critical leadership knowledge, skills, and dispositions required, but they should also develop strategies for assessing the performance of leadership candidates and gauging their progress toward demonstrating these critical competencies in real school settings.

To build the capacity of leadership candidates to assume second-order change responsibilities, programs must consider new approaches, interactions, and experiences that have a substantial likelihood of helping leaders develop the critical knowledge, skills, and dispositions needed. These changes will require tremendous commitments of time, energy, and resources. If, however, university preparation program leaders fail to respond to these challenges sincerely and aggressively, universities will suffer a loss of credibility across schools, school districts, and states. Scholars and practitioners with sincere commitments to social justice cannot ignore the costs of failing to share responsibility for the transformation of school leadership preparation programs. Universities, in partnership with districts and other partners, must strive to perfectly design a system of school leadership preparation that supports the attainment of educational excellence and equity in our schools.

Implications for School Districts

Practically every decision made by school boards, superintendents, and executive school district leaders will influence (positively or negatively) the capacity of school leaders to pursue and attain excellent and equitable learning results for students. Districts cannot simply "hire the right principal" and rely upon that individual to bring about the dramatic second-order changes needed to transform cultures, curricula, and instruction, especially when other district-level decisions complicate, obscure, negate, or draw resources and energy away from critical improvement efforts.

In our study of high-performing urban schools, we have noted substantial differences in the relationships between the high-performing schools identified and their district offices. In some situations, there is a clear and powerful connection between the efforts principals and other school leaders were making to improve culture, curricula, and instruction and the support provided by their districts. Perhaps, not surprisingly, these districts boast multiple schools that met the criteria for our National Excellence in Urban Education Award. Specifically, districts such as the Chula Vista Elementary School District and the Long Beach Unified School District in California, the Aldine Independent School District and the Brownsville Independent School District in Texas, and the Roanoke City Public Schools in Virginia are among the districts where more schools have met our award criteria than might be anticipated (given district size). In these districts, principals and school leaders benefited from district systems and structures that made school-level, second-order changes easier to pursue and enact. For example, it was much easier for school leaders to develop and sustain strong structures for regular teacher collaboration in districts that supported and encouraged such collaboration (the dedication of time, professional development, and other fiscal support) than it was in districts where leaders either bargained away opportunities for principals to dedicate time for teacher collaboration or consumed what should have been teacher collaboration time with district meetings.

We also identified many high-performing urban schools where district leaders were sincerely and justifiably pleased with the learning results generated, but nonetheless had limited understanding of the coherent educational improvement systems we found within their schools. In those situations, district leaders acknowledged repeatedly the great leaders and outstanding teachers in the award-winning schools, but they were not able to articulate a vision for ensuring that more of their urban schools would have great leaders and outstanding teachers who achieved similar or better results.

It should also be acknowledged that some of the schools that met our award criteria achieved their successes, in part, because their school leaders were able to bring about second-order changes in spite of district policies and decisions. For example, one principal from an award-winning school confided, "I try to do all the things our district office requires, but honestly, I have to give my teachers permission to focus on what will make sense for our students."

The quality and quantity of district support influenced the likelihood that school leaders could create and then sustain excellent and equitable learning results. Some of the schools awarded have retained strong learning results for 10 years or longer, in spite of principal turnover, changes in district leadership, and changes in state standards and assessments. On the other hand, it is sad to note that some of the schools we awarded several years ago show little evidence of their former excellence. We believe that the presence or lack of district support is a major variable in influencing the development and retention of high-performing urban schools.

District leaders (school boards, superintendents, and executive district leaders) are not likely to develop, support, and retain high-performing urban schools if they do not understand the factors that influence excellent and equitable learning results. District leaders should understand how culture, curricula, and instruction could be empowering school characteristics when designed to promote excellence and equity. District leaders should understand the centrality of supporting a coherent system of educational improvement focused on specific important outcomes. As well, district leaders need to understand the leadership challenges every school leader must face, as he or she seeks to bring about second-order changes. Without this knowledge, it will be difficult for district leaders to know how to support school leaders in creating high-performing schools. In fact, without this knowledge, it will be difficult for district leaders to stay out of the way of school leaders who have some capacity to advance excellent and equitable learning results in schools.

There is little in our current public education system designed to help school boards, superintendents, or executive district leaders develop any understanding of high-performing urban schools. Many district leaders have never stepped onto the campus of a high-performing urban school, interviewed a principal from a high-performing school, or spent time considering how their district policies, procedures, and programs either enhance or subvert critical school-level changes. There is substantial room for state education agencies, professional associations, and universities to play a role in building the capacity of district leaders in this regard. In this case, it might be hard to say that the system is perfectly designed to achieve current results, because, in truth, there is little semblance of a system. If we, as a nation, want excellent and equitable learning results for all of our children, we must perfectly design a system that ensures that the individuals who govern our schools and provide executive leadership know how to support school leaders in making essential second-order changes.

References

Argyris, C., Putnam, R., & Smith, D. M. (1985). *Action science: Concepts, methods, and skills for research and intervention.* San Francisco, CA: Jossey-Bass.

Argyris, C., & Schön, D. A. (1974). *Theory in practice: Increasing professional effectiveness.* San Francisco, CA: Jossey-Bass.

Carr, S. (July–August 2008). Editor's notebook: A quotation with a life of its own. *Patient Safety and Quality Healthcare.* Retrieved from http://psqh.com/editor-s-notebook-a-quotation-with-a-life-of-its-own.

Appendix A
2017 National Excellence in Urban Education Eligibility Criteria

The National Excellence in Urban Education Award (NEUE) is presented annually to the nation's highest performing urban schools. In May 2017, the National Center for Urban School Transformation (NCUST) will present this award to elementary schools, middle schools, high schools, and alternative schools. In order to compete for a National Excellence in Urban Education Award, schools must meet or exceed the following criteria.

General Criteria

1. **Urban Location:** The school must be located in a metropolitan area with 50,000 or more residents.

2. **Non-Selective Admissions:** In general, the school may not require students to meet academic criteria in order to attain or retain admission. For example, a school that requires students to possess/maintain a certain test score or possess/maintain a minimum grade point average would not be eligible for consideration. Schools may house programs (e.g., programs for students identified as gifted or talented) that admit children from beyond the school's attendance area through selective admissions if fewer than 10 percent of the school's students are enrolled through selective admissions.

3. **Low-Income Eligibility:** For elementary schools in which the highest grade is grade six or lower, at least 60 percent of the students enrolled (both in the prior and the current year) must have met eligibility criteria for free- or reduced-price lunch. For middle schools (grade nine or lower), at least 50 percent of the students must have met the same criteria. In high schools, at least 40 percent of the students must have met the same criteria.

4. **High Rates of Academic Proficiency:** The school must be able to demonstrate that the percentage of students demonstrating proficiency on state assessments, in both 2015 and 2016, was higher than the average of all schools in the state (within the same grade span grouping). The school must have exceeded the state average in at least half of the

subject areas/grade levels assessed in 2015 and 2016. *NOTE: In states where rates of academic proficiency are not being tabulated in 2016 because of new assessments, NCUST will use 2014 and 2015 data to assess this criterion. In states where rates of academic proficiency were not tabulated in 2015 because of new assessments, NCUST will use 2016 assessment data only. This note applies to items 4 through 7.*

5. **High Rates of Academic Proficiency for Every Racial/Ethnic Group:** The school must indicate the percentage of students from each racial/ethnic group who achieved academic proficiency. The school may be eligible to compete only if, in at least two academic subjects, the percentage of students proficient in each racial/ethnic group exceeds the average of all schools in the state.

6. **Evidence of High Achievement for English Learners:** If more than 20 students are identified as English learners, the school must present evidence that a high percentage of English learners are progressing toward proficiency with the English language. As well, the school must present evidence that a high percentage of English learners are achieving greater proficiency in at least two academic subjects.

7. **Evidence of High Achievement for Students with Disabilities:** The school must present evidence that a high percentage of students with disabilities are achieving greater proficiency in at least two academic subjects. Evidence must include the percentage of students with disabilities demonstrating proficiency on state assessments, but might also include evidence of students with disabilities demonstrating year-to-year achievement gains on state assessments or other indicators of success.

8. **Excellence in Science, Technology, Engineering, and Mathematics Education (STEM):** Each school must present evidence that their students are developing strong levels of success in STEM subjects.

9. **High Attendance Rates:** The school must have evidence to indicate that the average student attendance rate exceeded 92 percent for each of the past two academic years.

10. **Low Rates of Out-of-School Suspension:** The total number of days students were out of school because of suspensions must be smaller than the total number of students enrolled. Similarly, there must be a low rate of suspension for every racial/ethnic group of students.

11. **Evidence of Student Success at Subsequent Levels:** Each school must present evidence that their students achieve strong levels of academic success at the subsequent school level (e.g., elementary schools must show evidence that their students are successful at the middle school level; middle schools must show evidence that their students are successful at high school).

Additional Criteria for High Schools

In addition to the general criteria, high schools must meet the following criteria:

12. **Percentage of First-Year High School Students Advancing to the Second Year:** Each high school must present the number and percentage of their 2015–2016 first-year students (typically freshmen) who earned sufficient credit to be promoted to second-year status (typically sophomores).

13. **Percentage of Students Earning College Credit or Participating in Advanced Placement Courses during High School:** Each school must present evidence of the number and percentage of students who earned college credit in the prior year. Also, each applicant must present evidence of the number and percentage of students who participated in advanced placement or International Baccalaureate courses; the number and percentage who took advanced placement, International Baccalaureate, or Cambridge assessments; and the number and percentage who received passing scores.

14. **High Graduation Rates:** Each high school must present the latest four-year adjusted cohort graduation rate (as defined by the U.S. Department of Education). The four-year adjusted cohort graduation rate must be at least 70 percent for every racial/ethnic group of students.

15. **Number of Dropouts Recovered:** Each school must present data regarding the number of dropouts they helped re-enter into school. As well, schools must present data indicating the success of recovered students in earning credits and graduating.

Criteria for Alternative Schools

Alternative school applicants must meet criteria 1–3 above. Regarding item 2, alternative schools may be considered if they selectively enroll students who have experienced academic and behavioral difficulty in typical schools. Additionally, alternative schools must present data regarding all other criteria (4–15); however, there are no minimal eligibility criteria associated with these items. Alternative schools will be reviewed and considered on a competitive basis.

Appendix B
National Excellence in Urban Education Award Winners

Alabama

◆ **Birmingham City Schools** (Birmingham, AL)

Glen Iris Elementary (2013)

◆ **Dothan City Schools** (Dothan, AL)

Morris Slingluff Elementary (2013)

Arizona

◆ **Phoenix Elementary School District** (Phoenix, AZ)

Magnet Traditional School (2013)

◆ **Tucson Unified** (Tuscon, AZ)

C.E. Rose Elementary (2012)

California

◆ **Bakersfield City School District** (Bakersfield, CA)

Franklin Elementary School (2008)

◆ **Centinela Valley High School District** (Lawndale, CA–Los Angeles)

Lawndale High School (2009)

◆ **Chula Vista Elementary School District** (Chula Vista, CA)

Feaster Charter School (2015)

Hilltop Drive Elementary (2016)

Lauderbach Elementary (2012, 2016)

Montgomery Elementary (2012)

Mueller Charter (2012)

Myrtle S. Finney Elementary (2016)

Otay Elementary (2012)

♦ **Compton Unified School District** (Compton, CA)

Bursch Elementary (2009)

♦ **Cucamonga School District** (Rancho Cucamonga, CA–San Bernardino)

Rancho Cucamonga Middle School (2007)

♦ **Excellence and Justice in Education Academy** (El Cajon, CA)

Excellence and Justice in Education Academy

♦ **Garden Grove Unified School District** (Garden Grove, CA)

John A. Murdy School (2015)

♦ **Glendale Unified School District** (Glendale, CA)

Cerritos Elementary (2015)

Columbus Elementary (2012)

Horace Mann Elementary (2010, 2016)

♦ **KIPP Charter** (San Diego, CA)

KIPP Adelante Academy (2009)

♦ **Long Beach Unified School District** (Long Beach, CA)

International Elementary (2010)

Signal Hill Elementary (2008)

Thomas Edison Elementary (2007)

Tucker Elementary (2008)

♦ **Los Angeles Unified School District** (Los Angeles, CA)

Lemay Elementary (2010)

Nueva Vista Elementary (2010)

Synergy Charter Academy (2013)

♦ **Montebello Unified School District** (Montebello, CA–Los Angeles)

Montebello Gardens Elementary (2009)

♦ **National School District** (National City, CA—San Diego)

Ira Harbison School (2009)

♦ **Sacramento City Unified School District** (Sacramento, CA)

Golden Empire Elementary (2009)

♦ **San Bernardino City Unified School District** (San Bernardino, CA)

Hillside University Demonstration School (2016)

♦ **San Diego Unified School District** (San Diego, CA)

Kearny High School of International Business (2009)

The O'Farrell Charter School (2015)

♦ **Santa Ana Unified** (Santa Ana, CA)

Jim Thorpe Fundamental Academy (2012)

♦ **Sweetwater Union High School District** (National City, CA)

Granger Junior High School (2013)

National City Middle School (2012)

Florida

♦ **Broward County Public Schools** (Fort Lauderdale, FL)

William Dandy Middle School (2008, 2012)

♦ **Hillsborough County Public Schools** (Tampa, FL)

Muller Elementary (2006)

♦ **Miami-Dade County Public Schools** (Miami, FL)

Southside Elementary Museums Magnet School (2008)

Georgia

♦ **Atlanta Public Schools** (Atlanta, GA)

Charles L. Gideons Elementary (2007)

West Manor Elementary (2014)

Whitefoord Elementary (2010)

♦ **Gwinnett County Public Schools** (Duluth, GA)

Harris Elementary (2015)

Illinois

♦ **Chicago Public Schools** (Chicago, IL)

George Washington Elementary (2014, 2015)

♦ **Peoria Public Schools** (Peoria, IL)

Whittier Primary School (2006)

Kansas

♦ **Wichita Public Schools** (Wichita, KS)

Horace Mann Dual Language Magnet (2010)

Maryland

♦ **Montgomery County Public Schools** (Silver Spring, MD)
Highland Elementary School (2010)

Massachusetts

♦ **Lawrence Public Schools** (Lawrence, MA)
Community Day Charter Public School (2006)

♦ **Revere Public Schools** (Revere, MA)
Revere High School (2014)

Michigan

♦ **Detroit Edison Public Charter School** (Detroit, MI)
Detroit Edison Public School Academy (2007)

Missouri

♦ **Center School District** (Kansas City, MO)
Boone Elementary (2013)

♦ **Maplewood Richmond Heights Schools** (Maplewood, MO)
Maplewood Richmond Heights High School (2015)

New Jersey

♦ **Newark Public Schools** (Newark, NJ)
Branch Brook School (2010)
Harriet Tubman Blue Ribbon School (2008)

New York

♦ **Mount Vernon Public Schools** (Mount Vernon, NY–NYC)
Cecil H. Parker Elementary School (2007)

♦ **NYC Dept. of Education** (Bronx, NY)
Marble Hill High School for International Studies District #10 (2010)

♦ **Rochester City School District** (Rochester, NY)
Dr. Charles T. Lunsford School #19 (2010)
World of Inquiry Elementary (2009)

North Carolina

- **Charlotte-Mecklenburg Schools** (Charlotte, NC)
  Mallard Creek High School

- **Durham School District** (Durham, NC)
  R. N. Harris Integrated Arts/Core Knowledge School (2012)

Ohio

- **Cleveland Metropolitan School District** (Cleveland, OH)
  Louisa May Alcott Elementary School (2008)
  MC² STEM High (2012)
  Riverside School (2013)
  William Cullen Bryant Middle (2012)

- **Columbus Public Schools** (Columbus, OH)
  Columbus Alternative High School (2007)

- **Dayton Public Schools** (Dayton, OH)
  Dayton Business Technology High School (2013)

Oklahoma

- **Oklahoma City Public Schools** (Oklahoma City, OK)
  Linwood Elementary (2006)

Oregon

- **Self Enhancement Inc.** (Portland, OR)
  Self Enhancement Inc. Academy (2015)

Pennsylvania

- **School District of Philadelphia** (Philadelphia, PA)
  Bridesburg Elementary (2008)
  Franklin Towne Charter High School (2009)

Tennessee

- **Metropolitan Nashville Public Schools** (Nashville, TN)
  Rose Park Math and Science Magnet (2013)

Texas

- ◆ **Aldine Independent School District** (Houston, TX)

  A. B. Anderson Academy (2015)

  Aldine 9th Grade School (2013)

  Ernest F. Mendel Elementary (2013)

  Hambrick Middle School (2010)

  MacArthur Senior High School (2008, 2013)

  Mary Walke Stephens Elementary (2010, 2015)

  Stehlik Intermediate (2013)

- ◆ **Austin Independent School District** (Austin, TX)

  Dorinda L. Pillow Elementary School (2007)

- ◆ **Brownsville Independent School District** (Brownsville, TX)

  A. X. Benavides Elementary (2015, 2016)

  Daniel Breeden Elementary (2015, 2016)

  James Pace Early College High School (2016)

  U.S. Congressman Solomon P. Ortiz Elementary (2015)

  Veterans Memorial Early College High School (2016)

- ◆ **Dallas Independent School District** (Dallas, TX)

  James B. Bonham Elementary School (2009)

  Jimmie Tyler Brashear Elementary (2015)

  John J. Pershing Elementary (2015)

  John Quincy Adams Elementary (2015)

  Nathan Adams Elementary (2010)

  Trinidad Garza Early College High School (2012)

  Walnut Hill Elementary (2015)

- ◆ **Fort Worth Independent School District** (Fort Worth, TX)

  Charles A. Nash Elementary (2015)

  North Hi Mount Elementary (2015)

  Paul Laurence Dunbar Young Men's Leadership Academy (2015)

  South Hi Mount Elementary School (2016)

  W. C. Stripling Middle School (2015, 2016)

  W. P. McLean Middle School (2016)

- ◆ **Galena Park Independent School District** (Houston, TX)
  Tice Elementary (2013)
- ◆ **Garland Independent School District** (Garland, TX)
  Spring Creek Elementary School (2016)
- ◆ **Houston Independent School District** (Houston, TX)
  George Sanchez Elementary (2014, 2015)
  Sylvan Rodriguez Elementary (2014)
- ◆ **Pasadena Independent School District** (Pasadena, TX)
  Thompson Intermediate School (2014)
- ◆ **Sharyland Independent School District** (Mission, TX)
  B. L. Gray Junior High School (2015)
- ◆ **Socorro Independent School District** (El Paso, TX)
  Escontrias Elementary (2010, 2014)
  Mission Early College High School (2016)
  Spc. Rafael Hernando III Middle School (2016)
- ◆ **Uplift Education Charter School Network** (Dallas, TX)
  Uplift Education-Peak Prep (2012)
- ◆ **Ysleta Independent School District** (El Paso, TX)
  Eastwood Middle (2013, 2014)

Virginia

- ◆ **Manassas City Public Schools** (Manassas, VA)
  Weems Elementary (2015)
- ◆ **Norfolk Public Schools** (Norfolk, VA)
  Dreamkeepers Academy at J. J. Roberts Elementary (2008)
- ◆ **Richmond Public Schools** (Richmond, VA)
  Ginter Park Elementary (2006)
  Thomas H. Henderson Middle School (2008)
- ◆ **Roanoke City Public Schools** (Roanoke, VA)
  Fallon Park Elementary (2009)
  Preston Park Elementary (2014)
  Wasena Elementary (2015)

Washington, DC

♦ **Thurgood Marshall Academy Public Charter High School** (Washington, DC)

Thurgood Marshall Academy Public Charter High School (2014)